Bibliographic information published by the German National Library:

The German National Library lists this publication in the National Bibliography; detailed bibliographic data are available on the Internet at http://dnb.dnb.de .

Imprint:

Copyright © 2017 GRIN Verlag
Print and binding: Books on Demand GmbH, Norderstedt Germany
ISBN: 9783668738355

This book at GRIN:

https://www.grin.com/document/426831

Rohan Ahmed

Fraud Detection in White-Collar Crime

GRIN Verlag

GRIN - Your knowledge has value

Since its foundation in 1998, GRIN has specialized in publishing academic texts by students, college teachers and other academics as e-book and printed book. The website www.grin.com is an ideal platform for presenting term papers, final papers, scientific essays, dissertations and specialist books.

Visit us on the internet:

http://www.grin.com/

http://www.facebook.com/grincom

http://www.twitter.com/grin_com

Hochschule Heilbronn

Fraud Detection in White-Collar Crime

Bachelor thesis
for obtaining the academic degree of

**Bachelor of Science
(B.Sc.)**

in course of studies Information Systems
at the University of Heilbronn

submitted by Rohan Ahmed

Heilbronn, 4th December 2017

Dedication

This thesis is proudly dedicated to ...

ALL MY BELOVED FAMILY

(my mother, my father, my grandma,

my sisters and my lovely wife)

Thank for your endless love, prayers and support.

Management Summary

White-collar crime is and has always been an urgent issue for the society. In recent years, white-collar crime has increased dramatically by technological advances. The studies show that companies are affected annually by corruption, balance-sheet manipulation, embezzlement, criminal insolvency and other economic crimes. The companies are usually unable to identify the damage caused by fraudulent activities. To prevent fraud, companies have the opportunity to use intelligent IT approaches. The data analyst or the investigator can use the data which is stored digitally in today's world to detect fraud.

In the age of Big Data, digital information is increasing enormously. Storage is cheap today and no longer a limited medium. The estimates assume that today up to 80 percent of all operational information is stored in the form of unstructured text documents. This bachelor thesis examines Data Mining and Text Mining as intelligent IT approaches for fraud detection in white-collar crime. Text Mining is related to Data Mining. For a differentiation, the source of the information and the structure is important. Text Mining is mainly concerned with weak- or unstructured data, while Data Mining often relies on structured sources.

At the beginning of this bachelor thesis, an insight is first given on white-collar crime. For this purpose, the three essential tasks of a fraud management are discussed. Based on the fraud triangle of Cressey it is showed which conditions need to come together so that an offender commits a fraudulent act. Following, some well-known types of white-collar crime are considered in more detail.

Text Mining approach was used to demonstrate how to extract potentially useful knowledge from unstructured text. For this purpose, two self-generated e-mails were converted into structured format. Moreover, a case study will be conducted on fraud detection in credit card dataset. The dataset contains legitimate and fraudulent transactions. Based on a literature research, Data Mining techniques are selected and then applied on the dataset by using various sampling techniques and hyperparameter optimization with the goal to identify correctly predicted fraudulent transactions. The CRISP-DM reference model was used as a methodical procedure.

The results from the case study show, that Naïve Bayes and Logistic Regression in small datasets and Support Vector Machine as well as Neural Networks are appropriate Data Mining techniques to detect fraud. The results were measured using several evaluation metrics such as precision, accuracy, recall and F-1 score. The data analyst has the opportunity to improve the predictive accuracy by tuning the hyperparameters.

Text Mining can extract patterns and structures as well as useful information in text documents with the help of linguistic, statistical and mathematical methods. However, using Text Mining in unstructured data is difficult and time-consuming.

Contents

List of figures

List of tables

List of abbreviations

BKA	Bundeskriminalamt (engl. German Federal Office of Crime Investigation)
CGMA	Chartered Global Management Accountant
CIMA	Chartered Institute of Management Accountants
CM	Confusion Matrix
CRISP-DM	Cross-industry Standard Process for Data Mining
CV	Cross-Validation
DM	Data Mining
DT	Decision Tree
ICS	Internal Control System
IE	Information Extraction
IPPF	International Planned Parenthood Federation
IR	Information Retrieval
LR	Logistic Regression
MLP	Multilayer perceptron
NB	Naïve Bayes
NN	Neural Network
NLP	Natural Language Processing
RF	Random Forest
SVM	Support Vector Machine
TF	Term Frequency
TF-IDF	Term Frequency – Inverse Document Frequency
VSM	Vector Space Model
WB	Web Mining
WWW	World Wide Web

1 Introduction

1.1 Motivation and problem statement

White-collar crime is a current topic in business dealings. Due to economic change, white-collar crime is attracting a lot of media attention. Headlines about the fraudulent acts such as: "Top Manager cause a major part of white-collar crime"[1], "Fraudsters capture over 100 million euros with CEO-Fraud"[2] and "Credit card fraud alerts are on the rise — save yourself"[3] are therefore not uncommon for the audience. The current KMPG white-collar crime study shows, that every third company in Germany has been affected by white-collar crime in the last two years and even every second in big companies (KPMG, 2016: 7). According to the federal situation survey of Federal Criminal Police Office (Bundeskriminalamt -BKA), a total of 57.546 cases of white-collar crime were registered in 2016, which caused a loss of 2.970 million euros (BKA, 2016: 3-4).

Due the continuously growing amount of data, the number of white-collar crimes cases increases. Structural changes in different divisions and reorganizing business create new incentives and opportunities for white-collar crimes. It is becoming increasingly difficult for managers and annual auditors to extract information to detect fraud. Today, more than 30.000 gigabytes of data are generated every second – and the number is rising (Warren and Marz 2015: 1). Even in a company, large amount of data is generated daily, which are stored in various forms. This includes not only data stored in a relational database, but also data which is available in a semi-structured or unstructured from (e.g. PDF, XML's, e-mails).

Data mining (DM) is one of the analytics methods of business analytics and is used for pattern recognition in large data files. Based on past fraud cases, patterns are automatically identified that indicate untypical behaviour and anomalies. These patterns are then applied to existing databases to identify fraud cases that have similar characteristics.
Text Mining (TM) is used in comparison to DM for semi-structured and unstructured data to transfer this data into a structured form. TM is also used to unify and rationalize data sets, as well as to identify patterns and relationships in unstructured data.

---

[1] Spiegel Online, 2017 (translated from German)
[2] FAZ, 2017 (translated from German)
[3] New York Post, 2017

1.2   Research Methodology

In this bachelor thesis, a literature analysis according to the procedure of Webster & Watson is carried out. The following literature databases were used during the literature search:
- Google Scholar
- SpringerLink
- IEEE Xplore Digital Library
- ScienceDirect

To find relevant literatures following combinations of keywords were used: *White-collar crime, Fraud Detection, Machine Learning, Big Data, structured Data, unstructured Data, Data Mining and Text Mining.* To expand the search, another search was carried out with equivalent German terms. It has been noted, that synonyms were used for the keyword *White-collar crime* in many literatures. Therefore, the following two synonyms for *White-collar crime* were included in the literature search: *Fraud and economic crime.*

To find the most relevant literatures the search in databases was restricted to *Abstract, Title and Keywords*. Also, only literatures which had been published since 2000 were selected and only documents on which access was guaranteed were considered. In addition, the duplicates were removed from the search results. This was followed by a rough examination of the Abstracts. Results that have no relevance to the topics covered in this thesis and results that did not conform the formal standards of scientific work were removed. The remaining results were subjected to a more detailed substantive examination. Finally, the bibliographies of the results were searched for further relevant literature. The entire procedure is visualized in Figure 1 as a process.

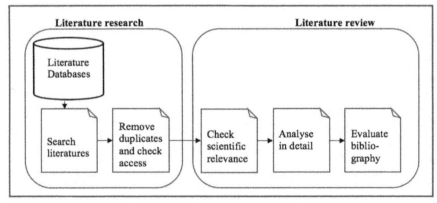

Figure 1: Procedure for literature analysis

1.3 Goal and structure of the thesis

The aim of this work is to find an answer to the following research question:

Which Data Mining techniques are appropriate for detecting white-collar crimes in structured and unstructured data?

To find an answer to this research question, this bachelor thesis is divided into six chapters. At the beginning of the thesis, the motivation and the problem statement are described as well as the relevance of the work is clarified.

Chapter 2 gives an overview of white-collar crime. To give the reader an insight into white-collar crime, some possible components of Fraud Management are discussed first in this chapter. Furthermore, significant explanatory approaches of fraud are shown. For this, special emphasis is placed on the Fraud Triangle by Cressey. Here, the offender and their motives, the emergence of white-collar crime and the damage caused by fraud are clearly in focus. With the help of literatures, studies and statistics some well-known white-collar crimes focused on financial fraud are pointed out and discussed in chapter 3.

The fourth chapter is divided into three parts: Big Data, Data Mining and Text Mining. After a brief introduction of Big Data and introducing various data formats, the importance of machine learning in fraud detection with the use of Data Mining and Text Mining is presented. The subchapter of Data Mining deals with types of machine learning and classification of data mining applications. The subchapter of Text Mining covers the seven practise areas of Text Mining and shows by means of an example how unstructured data can be transformed in a structured way to apply this data to predictive Data Mining techniques. For this purpose, two self-generated e-mails (spam / ham) will be converted into structured form with the help of the text classification procedure, term matrix and term frequency.

Chapter 5 is the centrepiece of this thesis. This chapter will cover a case study for fraud detection in credit card data. To implement the Data Mining project, the method of the CRISP-DM (Cross-Industry Standard Process for Data Mining) reference model consisting of six iterative steps is used.

CRISP-DM is an association of already well-established approaches such as the KDD (Knowledge Discovery in Databases) process and industrial approaches (e.g. SEMMA – Sample, Explore, Modify, Model and Assess) and is now regarded as a very popular method for increasing the success of DM projects (Moro and Laureano, 2011: 117; Wieland and Fischer, 2013: 48). CRISP-DM divides the DM process into six phases: Business Understanding, Data Understanding, Data Preparation, Modelling, Evaluation and Deployment (Shearer *et al.*, 2000: 13). Each phase describes individual generic tasks, regardless of the area of application and the used technologies, to carry out DM projects systematically (Wieland and Fischer, 2013: 48).

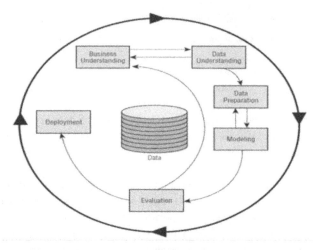

Figure 2: CRISP-DM reference model (Shafique and Qaiser, 2014: 219)

Business Understanding:

In the initial phase, the objective is to understand the project requirements and goals from a business perspective (Nadali, Kakhky and Nosratabadi, 2011: 162; Sharafi, 2013: 66). From this knowledge, a DM-problem is defined and a preliminary plan is created to achieve the objectives.

The case study in chapter 5 deals with fraud detection in credit card dataset. The used dataset has transactions of European cardholders made in the period of two days in 2013[4]. The goal is to detect fraudulent transactions by using DM techniques. To achieve this goal, various DM techniques will be used and compared with each other. It is important for banks to extract data from large datasets that can lead to fraud. This will give banks an idea of how high the losses inflicted on customers and the bank through fraud.

Data Understanding:

The second phase of the CRISP-DM is Data Understanding. In this phase, the data is collected, described, explored and the quality of the data is verified (Rocha and Júnior, 2010: 164).

Chapter 5.2 – Data Exploration covers the second phase of CRISP-DM – Data Understanding. The credit card dataset is therefore loaded with Pandas in Jupyter Notebook. The goal is to describe the data format, the amount of data, the number of records and fields in each table. The data exploration deals with the data mining questions, which are solved by query and visualization. This determines how many fraudulent and legitimate transactions are in the dataset and which features are relevant for the further investigation.

---

[4] Credit card fraud dataset available at: https://www.kaggle.com/dalpozz/creditcardfraud

Data Preparation:

The third phase in CRISP-DM is the Data Preparation. This phase includes all activities for creating the final dataset, which will be fed in the fourth phase of CRISP-DM – Modelling (Nadali, Kakhky and Nosratabadi, 2011: 162). The following activities can be assigned to this phase: select data, clean data, construct data, integrate data and format data (Shearer *et al.*, 2000: 16-17).

To prepare the datasets for the modelling phase, chapter 6.5 describes different sampling techniques. In this case study, the following sampling techniques are applied to the imbalanced dataset: Imbalanced data – no sampling technique is used for the first modelling phase; Undersampling - "Instances are randomly removed from the majority training set till the desired balanced is achieved" (Dubey *et al.*, 2014: 6); Oversampling – the data from the minority training set are duplicated until the desired balance is achieved (ibid.); SMOTE – the minority class is oversampled by creating synthetic examples in the neighborhood of the observed class (Dal Pozzolo, 2015: 37).

Furthermore, the data transformation step must be carried out in this phase to bring the data into a uniform scale. The normalization technique is used for this.

Modelling:

In this phase, various modelling techniques (DM-techniques) are selected and applied on the data, which is prepared in the data preparation phase (Sharafi, 2013: 66-67).

For the selection of DM techniques, a literature review was carried out in chapter 5.4. Based on the literature review, six DM techniques were selected, which were applied in the modelling phase. The selected DM techniques are: Logistic Regression, Random Forest, Support Vector Machine, Decision Trees, Neural Networks and Naïve Bayes. Sometimes it was necessary to stepping back in the data preparation phase to adjust the data. For example, after applying sampling techniques, shuffling was done to distribute the data in the data frame. The generation of test- and train set of data was also done at this phase. In chapter 5.6 different distribution combinations are applied on various DM techniques and the best one is selected.

Furthermore, hyperparameters were optimized in the undersampled dataset to improve the quality of DM techniques. For that, two hyperparameter optimization algorithms – Grid Search and Randomized Search – were compared with each other in chapter 5.11. Moreover, k-fold cross validation was applied to achieve an improvement (see chapter: 5.11.4).

Evaluation:

Evaluation is the fifth phase of CRISP-DM, "…which focuses on evaluation of obtained models and deciding of how to use the results" (Shafique and Qaiser, 2014: 220). The interpretation of the model depends on the algorithm. Models can be evaluated to verify whether the goals set in the business understanding phase are properly achieved or not (Sharafi, 2013:67 ; Shafique and Qaiser, 2014: 220).

In chapter 5.3 there are some model evaluation metrics, which are used in this case study to describe the performance of each classification model. Following metrics are included in a classification report: Recall, Precision, F1-Score and Accuracy. Confusion matrix is used to classify the number of true positive, true negative, false positive and false negative cases (Akosa, 2017: 2).

Deployment:

The last phase of the CRISP-DM process is Deployment. In this phase, the result and gained knowledge are mirrored back into the organization as the output of the analysis (Sharafi, 2013: 67). The following activities are assigned to the deployment phase: presentation of gained knowledge, deployment plan, plan of monitoring and maintenance, production of final report and project review (Shearer *et al.*, 2000: 18).

This bachelor thesis covers only a part of the deployment phase. The achieved goals of the case study as well as an evaluation summary and conclusion of the performance of each DM techniques are discussed in chapter 6.

The last chapter also includes a summary of the previous chapters, the answer to the research question, a critical review and an outlook on open issues that may be relevant for further research.

2 White-Collar Crime

The concept of White-collar crime was already conceived by Edward Alsworth Ross in 1907 (Salinger, 2004: 4). But it was Edwin Sutherland, who first published the term "White-Collar Crime" in 1937 (Stadler and Lovrich, 2012: 9). He defined the term as "a crime committed by a person of respectability and high social status in the course of his occupation" (Sutherland, 1983). Today his definition is somewhat outdated. There exists still no standard definition for the term white-collar crime but it is often used in literatures as a concept for various aspects of crime in the context of economic life (Techmeier, 2012). The concept is divided into two groups of crime: The internal criminality against his own company as occupational crime and corporate crime (Techmeier 2012: 13). What they have in common is their reference to the company (ibid.). The concept of white-collar crime of Sutherland is more related to the criminal behaviour in the economy to gain an individual benefit (Sutherland, 1983). On the other hand, occupational crime and corporate crime assume that corporations themselves commit a crime to pursue economic intentions (Techmeier 2012: 13).

In Germany, white-collar crime is the description for crime that have economic references (Schuchter, 2012: 44). As there is no legal definition of white-collar crime in Germany, BKA reverts to the catalog of § 74c para. 1 no. 1 to 6b of Judicature Act when assigning criminal offenses (BKA, 2015: 3). BKA defines white-collar crime as an abuse of criminal offenses in context of an actual or faked economic conformation which exploits the economic life process under profit-making leads to a loss of assets or damages many persons, other companies or the state (ibid.).

The study by KPMG (2016) found in a survey in the period from 2014 to 2016, that 36 percent of companies and 45 percent of large companies surveyed were effected by white-collar crime (KPMG, 2016: 6). It is difficult for companies to identify the damage caused during the period, because the preventive measures are missing (ibid.). To prevent white-collar crime, it is becoming increasingly important for companies to launch a compliance program (ibid.: 6-8). The survey found that despite high damage caused by white-collar crime, on third of the surveyed of companies are not ready to invest more than 10,000 euros in a compliance programs (ibid.: 7). To clarify white-collar crime, 57 percent of the surveyed companies are using the stored data for data analysis (ibid.). In large and medium-sized companies, an e-mail review is also carried out to detect white-collar crime (ibid.). Small companies rely to classical education measures, because of the lack of technical know-how and resources (ibid.).

2.1   Fraud Management

Establishing an effective internal control system (ICS) in a company is self-evident (Zawlilla et.al. 2012: 14). This means that regular checks can be carried out and the trust that is given can also be justified. It can reduce the risk of an employee who is thinking to commit a fraud (ibid.). Because of an ICS, it is possible to supervise an employee work for years and to compensate accordingly, so that they are satisfied. But, a worked and lived ICS is not sufficient enough to prevent fraud or to discover it very early (ibid.: 15). The ICS is known in Fraud Detection area to detect the irregularity as soon as possible after the act (ibid.). It is also interesting to know how a fraudulent activity can be detected before the act. The implementation of Prevention Fraud & Fraud Management is used in this content (ibid.). A better term for Fraud-Management would be the Anti-Fraud-Management, because this is ultimately to the defence, the fight against economic and corporate crime (Hofmann, 2008: 53-55). The Audit-Factory (2013) defines an Anti-Fraud-Management system "… as the purposeful bundling of functions and processes in a company…". A Fraud-Management-System includes three tasks: Fraud Prevention, Fraud Detection and Responding to Fraud (CIMA, 2009: 24 pp.). It is used in large companies as a company-wide system for the prevention, detection and adequate reaction of fraudulent acts (ibid.). In many literatures, the third approach "Responding to Fraud" based on an anti-fraud management concept is limited to the keyword "Fraud Investigation" (IPPF, 2009: 24 & CGMA, 2012: 19).

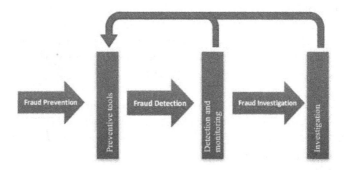

Figure 3: Prevention, Detection and Investigation of Fraud (IPPF, 2009: 19)

2.1.1   Fraud Prevention

Fraud prevention is understood to mean all measures which are concerned with the prevention of white-collar crimes. The prevention is responsible to discover the crime before the act happens (Zawlilla et. al., 2012: 263). The prevention of future oriented prevention of criminal offences must be at the centre of anti-fraud management (Hofmann, 2008: 81). Hoffman quoted from Gisler: „Preventing fraud is infinitely better than detecting afterwards and then struggling to recover from financial losses and negative publicity." (ibid.). The investment in prevention causes a lot of costs for the company and the benefits are difficult to measure (ibid.). Only if a company experiences a fraud case, the benefit of investment becomes tangible (ibid.). It should be considered that the damage caused by white-collar crime is much higher than the investment for prevention and detection.

For companies, the question arises, how they can archive best prevention. The first step could be for example an efficient internal control system and redesign of processes with the aim of achieving the highest level of security (Hofmann, 2008: 82). "An organization with effective internal controls deters fraudsters from the temptation to commit fraud" (IPPF, 2009: 20).
For this, companies should install effective and efficient instruments that can at least detect in an early stage that there has been a criminal offence (Hofmann, 2008: 82). According to the International Professional Practices Framework (IPPF, 2009: 20) the "Management is primarily responsible for establishing and maintaining internal controls in the organization".

2.1.2 Fraud Detection

The second approach of Fraud Management – Fraud Detection ensures that white-collar crimes are identified at an early stage (Zawlilla et. al. 2012: 264). Through the implementation of different measures, the detection quote can be increased, as well as a possible early detection time can be reached (ibid.). According to IPPF (2009: 21) "Detective controls are designed to provide warnings or evidence that fraud is occurring or has occurred". Zawlilla and other authors (2012: 265) mentions some specific measures that can be relevant to a fraud detection. For instance, there are measures like:

- Update Fraud Detection programs;
- Determine sample and standard analysis;
- Execute current analysis of risk vulnerability;
- Examine and clarify strikingly facts;
- Derive consequences and measures;
- and others.

2.1.3 Fraud Investigation

"Organizations investigate for possible fraud when there is a concern or suspicion of wrongdoing within the organization." (IPPF, 2009: 23). This is the third approach of a fraud management concept. Such a suspicion may result from a formal and informal complaint process, "… including an audit designed to test for fraud." (ibid.). "A fraud investigation consists of gathering sufficient information about specific details and performing those procedures necessary to determine whether fraud has occurred, the loss or exposures associated with the fraud, who was involved, and how it happened." (Gleim, 2008: 19). For investigation of fraud involves "… internal auditors, lawyers, investigators, security personnel, and other specialists…" (ibid.). The investigations must be prepared and documented so that they are effective in a possible legal process (ibid.).

A fraud response plan is "…an integral part of the organisation's contingency plans." (CGMA, 2012: 31). With it, the arrangements can be defined, which are provided for a detected or suspected fraud (ibid.: 44). "… (B)enefits arising from the publication of a corporate fraud response plan are its deterrence value of likelihood that it will reduce the tendency to panic." (ibid.). Other benefits can for example minimise losses of organizations and retain market confidence (ibid.: 19). A fraud response plan is a formal means by which all information can passed on to all employees and possibly to external persons, e.g. stakeholders and suppliers (CIMA, 2009: 44). The Management decides whether a fraud has occurred or not (ibid.). They are also responsible for the publish of a fraud investigation to extern organizations (IPPF, 2009: 23). A successful published examination may be a reminder for a person who, e.g. was on the way to commit a criminal offence (ibid.).

The investigation plan for Fraud Investigation is structured as follows: "The lead investigator determines the knowledge, skills, and other competencies needed to carry out the investigation effectively and assigns competent, appropriate people to the team." (IPPF, 2009: 24). The plan for the investigation may include (ibid.):
- Activities such as documentation and storage of evidence,
- "Determining the extent of fraud",
- "Determining the techniques used to perpetrate fraud",
- "Evaluating the cause of the fraud", and
- "Identifying the perpetrators" (ibid.).

2.2 Fraud Triangle
The concept of "Fraud Triangle" is introduced to the professional literature in SAS No. 99, Consideration of Fraud in a Financial Statement Audit (2002) and is now used in various ways, when the emergence of white-collar crime is presented. The fraud triangle is an explanation for the conditions which must be met for the commission of white-collar crime. This approach is based on the American criminologist and sociologist Donald R. Cressey (Scherp 2015: 85). He dealt with the causes of fraud in companies. The result of his thought is a simple and convincing model – the "Fraud Triangle" (ibid.).

Scherp (2015: 86) identifies three conditions of Fraud Triangle which should come together to enable a fraud:
- Opportunity
- Incentive/Pressure
- Rationalization/Attitude

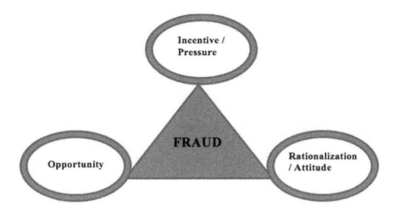

Figure 4: Fraud-Triangle (cf. Scherp, 2015)

2.2.1 Opportunity

The opportunity is the basic possibility of committing a criminal act without being caught. This includes the position of the offender in a company, which allows him to have access to object of the crime or to influence processes to abuse them on behalf of the company (Scherp 2015: 86). In this case two elements play a particular role. On the one hand, the individual's Basis-Know-How of the potential offender, on the other hand, his technical skills are important (ibid.). The first element 'Knowledge' includes e.g. the knowledge, functionality and weaknesses of ICS, the knowledge of the deliberate action of others, or the recognition that the employer's trust in one's own person can be used for his own benefit (ibid.). The technical skills are those which are necessary for the actual execution of the action. These are usually skills such as methodological or professional skills. From this it follows that, generally using the function of the employee, the manner of crime is essentially predetermined (ibid).

2.2.2 Incentive/Pressure

To commit a fraudulent act, the offender must have an incentive or should be under a pressure. The existence of a fraudulent motivation exists, if the financial stability of the company overall or the personal financial situation of the management is threatened or if the pressure to meet the expectations of third parties is particularly pronounced (Hofmann 2008: 207). Even cases of the conscious and intentional mere injury to the employer without self-interest are sometimes present (Scherp 2015: 87). Through fraudulent actions in the banking sector and fraud to customers, the offender like to achieve the best sales figures for his company (ibid.). In early researches of Cressey, he assumed, that criminals are involved into fraudulent activities by a specific pressure situation (ibid.: 88). But it was very quickly clear, that there might be autonomous motives or intrinsic motivations for fraudulent activities, such as Financial

Pressure and Perceived Pressure (ibid.). But also, the "Greed" is a significant motivation to achieve indirect benefits such as bonus, promotion, recognition and career (ibid: 87).

2.2.3 Rationalization/Attitude

Rationalization is the final component of component to complete the fraud triangle. "Rationalization is how the fraudster justifies inappropriate actions. It is 'the provision of reasons to explain to oneself or others behavior for which one's real motives are different and unknown or unconscious.'" (Biegelman and Bartow 2012: 35). Using internal justification, the fraudster can maintain his self-image as a valuable member of society, so that "the fraudster is convinced that what occurred is not bad or wrong. (…) Rather than consider themselves as criminals who just defrauded their company, they make themselves into victims." (ibid). Classical inner justifications are a self-image as essentially non-criminal personality and the existence of subjective justifications. The fraudsters reflect instead, 'It is my money anyway or I have borrowed the money only …' etc. The creepy part here is that rationalization takes place in the mind of the fraudster and is not visible.

3 Types of White-Collar-Crimes

3.1 Fraud

The term fraud can be understood and defined in different ways. There exists no universal definition of fraud. According to Singleton (2010: 40) "Fraud is a generic term, and embraces all the multifarious means that human ingenuity can devise, which are resorted to by one individual, to get an advantage by false means or representations." He also defines Fraud as deception (ibid.). "One might say that fraud in the form of intentional deception (including lying and cheating) is the opposite of truth, justice, fairness, and equity." (ibid.).

Ngai et al. (2011: 562) describe two different definitions. The first definition is in relation to The Oxford English Dictionary (2017), which defines fraud as a "Wrongful or criminal deception intended to result in financial or personal gain." The second definition mentioned is from Ngai et al. (2011: 562) who describes, "fraud as leading to abuse of a profit organization's system without necessarily leading to direct leading consequences".

Fraud can be classified as an internal fraud or as an external fraud (Jans et al. , 2009: 3 from Bologna and Lindquist, 1995). Examples of an external fraud can be providers, suppliers, or contractors (ibid.). On the other hand, the activities of managers in an organization that commit a criminal offense are referred as internal fraud. But a combination of an internal and external fraud can also occur when, for example, an employee cooperates with an external to take financial advantages and harm the organization (ibid.). Furthermore, after Bologna and Lindquist (1995) other classifications of fraud are mentioned in the literature (Jans et al. , 2009: 3):

- Transaction Fraud versus Statement Fraud
- Fraud for and against the organization
- Management and Non-Management Fraud

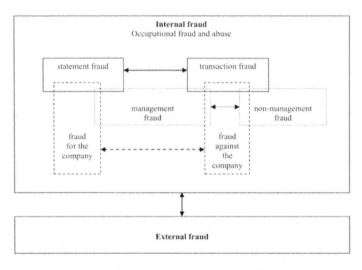

Figure 5: Fraud classification overview (Jans, Lybaert and Vanhoof, 2009: 5)

As shown in Figure 5, there is a distinction between internal and external fraud. All other represented classifications are assigned here to internal fraud. The two significant fraud types in internal fraud are "statement" and "transaction fraud". On the second level, there is a distinction between the "… occupation level of the fraudulent employee: management versus non-management fraud" (ibid: 5). Figure 5 also shows, that a manager can commit both types of statement and transaction fraud, a non-management is limited to transaction fraud. In the last classification, a difference is made between fraud for and against the company. Fraud for the company is assigned here to statement fraud, "(a)lthough fraud for the company does not necessarily need to be statement fraud (for example breaking environmental laws) …" (ibid.: 5-6).

The authors assume that "… only managers are in an advantageous position to commit fraud for the company…" (ibid.: 6), therefore an overlap with management fraud is presented in the figure above while fraud against the company can be committed by managers and not managers (ibid.).

In the following sub-chapters, some types of fraud and white-collar crimes are examined somewhat more closely. Before the examination, it is also important to mention, that the area of fraud is so large, that a separate elaboration can be made of it. Therefore, financial fraud is divided into three specific areas: Bank Fraud, Insurance Fraud and Security Fraud. For example, credit card fraud and money laundering can be assigned to bank fraud. On the other hand, health care fraud and automobile fraud can be attributed to insurance fraud. There are many types of financial fraud and other white-collar crimes. This thesis focuses on the most common types of them.

3.2   Credit Card Fraud

Credit card fraud is the most common subcategory of Bank Fraud. The Legal Dictionary (n.d.) defined credit card fraud as "The unauthorized use of an individual's credit card or card information to make purchases, or to remove funds from the cardholder's account.". In this day and age, almost every person owns a credit card. On the one hand, the use of credit card makes life easier for us; on the other hand, frauds are more and more frequently detected which otherwise would not have existed. Brause et. al (2010: 1) estimate, that for 400,000 transactions a day, a reduction of only 2.5 percent can save millions a year.

Credit card fraud increased in 2014 in Germany according to FICO (2015). They report that a sample of 7.5 million active cards issued in Germany showed losses to credit card fraud up by 17 percent in the year from October 2013 to September 2014, compared to the previous year.

According to a report from Buonaguidi (2017) which was published by BBC on 12th July 2017, since "...1980s, there has been an impressive increase in credit, debit and pre-paid cards internationally." In Nilson's report (2016) which was referred by Buonaguidi, some numbers of credit card usage are displayed. In 2015, this payment systems generated world-wide more than 31 trillion dollars in total volume, up 7.3 percent from 2014 (ibid.). Fraud loss in 2015 amounted to 21.84 billion dollars, an increase of 20.6 percent compared to 2014 (Nilson, 2016: 1,6)

Buonaguidi (2017) also mentions the two most important categories of credit card fraud: card-notpresent and card-present-frauds. The first mentioned type of fraud is the most common. This can happen if the cardholder's information is stolen and used illegaly (ibid.). Such fraud-ulent information is usually obtained by so-called "phishing" emails (ibid.). But also, tele-phone and social networks are used to get financial information from the victim (Nilson, 2016: 6). Card present frauds are less common today. This type may occur, e.g. the cardholder loses his card and the fraudster uses it in a supermarket. The second known type is "skim-ming" (Buonaguidi, 2017). Here, the fraudster uses the card of the consumer and pushes it into a device which saves all information. If the fraudster now uses the data to make a pur-chase, the victim's account will debit.

3.3   Healthcare Fraud

Health care fraud, like other fraud, demands that false information is represented as truth. The Legal Dictionary (n.d.) defined health care fraud as "The knowing and wilful executing, or attempt to execute, a scheme or deceit to defraud a health care insurance or benefit program, or to obtain by fraudulent means any benefit or payment from the program." There are many possibilities for billing fraud in the health care system. For example, forging prescriptions, double billing, unnecessary treatments and misuse of insurance card are the most common types which are countinued to this fraud (Lescher and Baldeweg, 2012: 5). The Legal Information Institute and National Health Care Anti-Fraud Association (LII, n.d & NHCAA, n.d.) mention other forms that occur in a health care fraud. Some of these are:

- Billing for services that were never rendered-either or medically unnecessary services purely for the purpose of generating insurance payments,
- Obtaining fully covered medicines that the patient does not need and sell them on the black market to gain profit,
- Billing for expensive services or procedures that were not actually made, but patients were treated with more favourable resources,
- Intentional incorrect reporting of diagnoses or procedures to maximize payment,
- Falsification of diagnosis to perform tests of operations that are not medically necessary.

In a PwC study from Lescher and Baldeweg (2012: 5) on health care fraud, health policy makers, care providers, costumers and experts agree that the misconduct in the health care system causes annual outages. Therefore, insurance companies are forced to increase their insurance contributions (ibid.). Victims in this case are the citizens who must pay their increased health insurance. The PwC study points to the Anti-Corruption Transparency International Germany which assumes that fraud, waste and corruption in the health care caused damage in double-digit millions (in Europe) (ibid.). The European Network (EHFCN, 2010) reported a financial loss of 13 billion euro in 2010. This corresponds to around 5% of current health expenditure in Germany (Lescher and Baldeweg, 2012: 12). In Germany, health care can distinguish between the statutory health insurance and private health insurance. The PwC study (ibid.) transfers the above-mentioned loss totals to Germany and assumes that in year 2010 the private health insurance can be allocated 1-billion-euro loss. With the statutory health insurance, it can be assumed an 8-billion-euro damage by fraud (ibid.). The PwC study (ibid.) therefore estimates that the amount in the offense type billing fraud can be 100 to 200 million euros annually. The PwC survey reveals that almost every surveyed company is victim of billing fraud (ibid.). Approximately 64 percent of fraud cases were affected by statutory health insurance. They stated that in year 2011 one to ten cases of fraud occurred (ibid.). On the other hand, private health insurance companies identified between 11 and 50 cases of billing fraud (ibid.). It should be noted that only the numbers from the so-called bright field are mentioned here. The numbers of a large dark field are not known. Almost two-thirds, which corresponds to abut 62 percent of the companies surveyed, estimate that an unidentified fraud (dark field) is high or very high (ibid.).

3.4 Embezzlement

According to Böttner (n.d.) embezzlement is referred to as the second largest group of crime in law relating to economic offenses. The accusation of embezzlement can affect anyone who makes decisions about foreign assets (ibid.). They can be simple employees with thier own decision-making powers in addition to manage directors, board members and politicians (ibid.). In simple word, embezzlement means, personal use of money, property or some other value thing that has been entrusted to an offender's care or control. According to the German Criminal Code section 266a embezzlement is defined as „Whosoever abuses the power accorded him by statute, by commission of a public authority or legal transaction to dispose of assets of another or to make binding agreements for another, or violates his duty to safeguard the property interests of another incumbent upon him by reason of statute, commission of a public authority, legal transaction or fiduciary relationship, and thereby causes damage to the person, whose property interests he was responsible for ..." (Bohlander, 2016). Embezzlement of money is not always associated to white-collar crime, as in other cases. In most cases, embezzlement in area of white-collar crime always occurs where the management has company funds for private expenditure (Liebl, 2016: 5).

This type of offence occurs frequently in connection with the investment fraud (BKA, 2016: 4). The police criminal statistics show that in year 2016 the number of fraud and embezzlement cases fell by 2,6 % to 7815 cases. The result was a loss of 356 million euros (2015: 328 million euros) (ibid.: 14).

3.5   Criminal Insolvency Offences

Offenses involving indebtedness and the imminent insolvency of a debtor are referred to as criminal insolvency offences (Wolfhart Nitsch, 2014: 564). This crime also breaks the faith of the creditors and causes damage to the entire economy, or at least tries to do so. Insolvency means in generally language to use inability to pay (Diversy and Weyand, 2013: 21). There are two different types of insolvency proceedings that must be distinguished. The rule insolvency and customer insolvency (ibid.: 19). The rule insolvency is for persons with income from self-employment and for former self-employed persons with more than 20 creditors or debts from working conditions. Customer insolvency, on the other hand, is addressed to all other persons, such as jobholder, unemployed persons, pensioners etc.

The high number of insolvencies is an economic problem for years. Not only large companies, but also midsize companies as well as start-up companies are hit by business crashes. Creditreform (2016a) announces the number of insolvency in Germany for the year 2016 in a press release. They report, that the number of insolvencies has been declining for six years. In 2016, a total of 123,800 insolvency cases were registered. This is a 3 % less than in 2015 (127,500 cases). The number of customer insolvencies fell by 2,5 % in 2016. A total of 78,200 cases were registered in this year. In contrast to customer insolvencies, the number of rule insolvencies declined more with -6,4 %. A total of 21,700 rule insolvencies were registered in 2016 (2015: 23,180). This has reached the lowest level since 1999. (ibid.).
Furthermore, Creditreform (2016a) reports that the total of financial losses in 2016 has risen. In 2016, a total loss of around 27.5 billion euros was achieved, about 40 % more than in the previous year and the highest figure in four years. Also, about 221,000 workers were affected

by the insolvency of employers. The number of older companies (over 20 years old) who reported an insolvency has risen to 16,4 %. (ibid.).

The legal form of the private limited company is very popular in the German economic life and is often found in investigations of the company collapse (Diversy and Weyand, 2013: 21). The main reason for corporate crises is the small equity ratio, especially for companies in the services sector (ibid.: 22). For the incorporation of this legal form, only a small amount of capital is required, but it can be fully involved in economic use (ibid.: 23). According to another press release of Creditreform (2016b), the equity ratio in the midsize companies has continued to decline. It is due to the low interest rates that facilitate loan financing. A survey showed that only 29,3 % of respondents had an equity ratio of more than 30 %. In the previous year, it was 31,6 %. Less than 10 % of equity now has 29,8 % of respondents (2016: 28,5 %). In most cases, the cause of insolvency is the equity ratio. This usually applies to small companies that do not employee more than 5 people (Diversy and Weyand, 2013: 23). The new start-up companies are particularly vulnerable to crises, especially if the existence of subsidies eliminated or added unforeseen conditions (ibid.). This includes management failure caused by smaller family businesses and leading to corporate crises. But also, fixed costs as well as the dependence on individual customers, whose collapse leads to own damage, are among them (ibid.: 24). They try to save their company with all possible means by shifting the risks to lenders and try to save the remaining asset components (ibid.). Moreover, there is a fear of losing the social position thorough insolvency, which leads to an incentive to commit a crime, wanted or unwanted and to safe the current standard to living (ibid.).

3.6 Corruption

As with the term of white-collar crime, there is no legal definition for corruption in the German Criminal Code. It should also be noted, that corruption is, to certain extent, part of the economic offence. For example, cases such as bribe an official, e.g. handover of a banknote to a police officer to avoid the loss of his driving license, is not an economic offence. Transparancy International Deutschland e. V. (TID n.d.) describes corruption as abused of entrusted power for private benefit or advantage. Corruption can be caused by bribery or corruptibility in international business or in its own country. Likewise, the purchasability in politics or attempting to gain advantages through bribes is called corruption.

In the German Criminal Code (Bohlander 2016) a distinction is made between two criminal offences – the bribery in public sector (section 331ff, Criminal Code) and bribery in commercial sector (section 299ff, Criminal Code). Criminal statistics distinguish between situational and structural corruption. Situational corruption is understood to mean corruption practices which are spontaneously and not planned or prepared (Hlavica et. al., 2017: 227). Structural corruption is characterized by acts that are based on long-term corrupt relations and which are knowingly planned (ibid.).

An example of a typical corruption case in white-collar crime would be: If e.g. an official receives grants or gifts from a company, so that he gives the assignment for a renovation to this company.

A study by KMPG (2016:11) showed, that 48 % of companies surveyed consider the risk of corruption to be high. However, only 16 % of companies were affected by corruption in year 2015, which is 6 % less than in previous year (ibid.).

4 Data Mining, Text Mining and Big Data

4.1 Introduction into Big Data

With the increasing usage of electronic devices, especially smartphones, our daily life faces Big Data and new challenges. Thereby, it is also difficult for a data analyst to understand new problems and provide real-time solutions. To imagine well Sharma and Pandey (2015: 1) mention some well-known platforms, which consume high data volume: Twitter for example creates more than 12 terabytes daily, Facebook generates over 25 terabytes log data every day and at Google it is likewise 24,000 terabytes data each day.

A bigger problem of this massive data is that there are three different essential attributes of Big Data which make it difficult to understand. Around 80 percent of data are in unstructured or in semi-structured form (Talib *et al.*, 2016: 414), so "... there is a huge need to understand these unstructured data and solve many business problems as possible" (Sharma and Pandey, 2015: 1). Many companies have a common problem in their unstructured data which is the detection of financial frauds (ibid.: 4-6). It brings a lot of losses every year (see Chapter 3: Frauds and White-Collar-Crime). As said by Sharma and Pandey in their literature review (2015: 2), some experts divided the characteristics of data in four to five V's (ibid.). In the following sub-chapters of this thesis, only three main V's will be discussed.

4.1.1 The 3 V's of Big Data

Volume:

The large amount of data is considered as an important characteristic of Big Data. Sharma and Pandey (2015: 2) defined Volume as "...the amount of data one needs to process, to find meaningful information". McAfee and Brynjolfsson (2012: 61-68) assumed that since the beginning of 2012, about 2.5 Exabyte's (or circa 2.600.000 terabytes) of data were created each day and every 40 months the data doubled. Cano (2014) said that "Collecting and analyzing this data is clearly an engineering challenge of immensely proportions". It is also not possible to store the data on one place because of the size. Therefore, distributed systems are used which brought the data together by software if the analyzer needs them to analyze (ibid).

Velocity:

The high speeds at which the data is generated and processed are also a feature of Big Data. This is because of social media platforms like Facebook, Twitter and YouTube, because any person who has access to internet can create data on these platforms (Sharma and Pandey, 2015: 2). Therefore, with growing numbers of users, applications, networking and sensors, the data is always available faster and can also be processed in real-time (ibid.). That is not so long ago, batch-processing was common. It was normal to get an update from the database every night or every week because data processing took a lot of time (Van Rijmenam, 2015). "Today the speed at which data is created is almost unimaginable" (ibid.). Every minute people from all over the world upload hundred hours of a video on Youtube, every minute over 200 emails and on Twitter almost 300.000 tweets are sent (ibid.). These all need a database with a higher performance.

Variety:
Another important feature of Big Data is the heterogeneity of the data structure. Data is generating in various formats. "In the past, all data that was created was structured data..." and today "... 90% of the data is generated by organisation is unstructured data." (Van Rijmenam, 2015). Since the data is now generated from different sources, for example from social networks or sensors, they differ in their format. A distinction is made between structured, semi-structured and unstructured data (ibid.).

4.1.2 Data Forms

Structured Data:
These data come in a correct format and database schema. Structured data is often generated during a business transaction (Sharma and Pandey, 2015: 2-3). The results of the transactions are usually stored in a relational database, so that "... querying the data and then extracting relevant information is quite easy. This is how most of the organization keep their data with the well-defined database schema." (ibid.: 2).

Semi-Structured Data:
"These types of data also exist in a structured format, but data is not maintained in a database, rather flat files." (ibid.). The different definitions that exist for semi-structured data can be summarized as follows: Semi-structured data is not strictly typed, but has a certain structure, which cannot be recognized immediately. Examples for unstructured data are: xml data, JSON file and source code of a website in html format (ibid.).

Unstructured Data:
The unstructured data has not a unique structure and is stored outside of a conventional database system. In today's world, the most amounts of generated data are unstructured (ibid.: 2). A very high percentage of all data stored in a company computer system is in an unstructured form. Examples of such data are images, texts, phone calls and notes, which are generated almost daily in every company (ibid.). Other examples are shown in figure below.

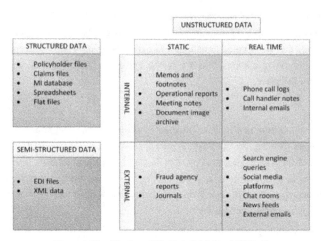

Figure 6: Classification of Big Data (Blakehead, 2013: 1)

As shown in the figure above, data is available in different formats. The three attributes, structured data, semi-structured data and unstructured data have already been briefly explained. The structured data and semi-structured data have an identifiable structure. On the other hand, the unstructured data comes in most varied forms, as can be seen in the figure above. In today's world, the analysis of unstructured data is a new challenge (Rashid Al-Azmi, 2013: 4)

These types of data play a very important role in the area of fraud detection. While the structured data can be analyzed easier by using different data mining techniques, the unstructured data in this area is a major problem. As mentioned in the chapter "Types of White-Collar Crimes" (see Chapter 3), there are many types of fraud that can create a high damage to the company or the state. To reduce the fraud, the data must be analyzed. However, since this data is kept in an unstructured form, the first challenge is to analyze the behavioral patterns to find the context. Text Mining (TM) is used for this purpose. "Text Mining is a process of extracting meaningful numeric indices (structured data) from unstructured text" (Gupta and Gill, 2012: 189) and "… can analyze words or cluster of words and can used for determining the relationship with other variables of interest such as fraud or non fraud." (ibid.)

4.2 Data Mining

Data Mining (DM) is part of machine learning techniques and is defined as the process of analysing large databases (Hashimi, Hafez and Mathkour, 2015: 729). DM also known as Knowledge Discovery is an automated process that analyses huge amounts of data to discover new information, hidden patterns and behaviours (ibid.). For DM, there exist no clear definition in the web. According to Gartner (2017), "Data mining is the process of discovering meaningful new correlations, patterns and trends by sifting through large amounts of data stored in repositories, using pattern recognition technologies as well as statistical and mathematical techniques."

DM techniques tend to learn models from data as well as most machine learning algorithms (Potamitis, 2013: 27). There are three approaches to the learning of data mining models: supervised learning, unsupervised learning and semi-supervised learning (Sorin, 2012: 110).

4.2.1 Types of Machine Learning

Supervised Learning method is used most frequently, where the model is trained with predefined class labels (Lloyd, Mohseni and Rebentrost, 2013: 1). Therefore, it is important in supervised learning, that the labels are known. For example, this method is most commonly used for credit card fraud detection, where the class labels are known as fraudulent and non-fraudulent transaction (Bhattacharyya, Jha, Tharakunnel, & Westland, 2011). The prediction model can be created with a training set. Each new transaction can be compared to the model to predict its class. If the new transaction is like fraudulent behaviour, as described by the trained model, it will be classified as a fraudulent transaction. Another important challenge for the supervised learning approach is that the class distribution is balanced for good predictions. For this purpose, various sample techniques are mentioned in the literature, such as undersampling and oversampling technique. These sampling techniques are considered in more detail in chapter 5.5 "Sampling techniques".

Compared to supervised learning, the goal of **unsupervised learning** is to find hidden structures in unlabeled data (Lloyd, Mohseni and Rebentrost, 2013: 1). A suitable DM approach for unsupervised learning is the clustering process.

The last approach of machine learning is **semi-supervised learning**. This method lies between supervised learning (all training data are available with labels) and unsupervised learning (all training data are available without labels) (Potamitis, 2013: 23). So, in this approach a small number of labelled samples and many unlabeled samples are required (ibid.).

4.2.2 Classification of Data Mining Applications

In the following, the most common approaches of data mining applications classes are described, which are also mentioned in the study by Sorin (2012: 115). The following applications of data mining can handle different classes of problems.

Classification:
Classification is the most commonly applied DM technique, which employs a set of preclassified examples to develop a model that can classify the population of records at large (Herbert, 1999: 10-11). The literature research (Zhang and Zhou, 2004: 34) says, that classification or prediction is the process of identifying a set of common features, and suggesting

differentiating models that describe and distinguish data classes and concepts based on an example. The most common DM techniques for fraud detection are Neural Networks, Decision Trees (DT) and Support Vector Machines (SVM) (Ngai *et al.*, 2011: 563).

Clustering:
In Clustering, as known as cluster analysis the groups of objects, which have a similarity, are identified (Ngai *et al.*, 2011: 563). The reason to choose the clustering procedure is, that some applications of the class affiliation is not available or costly to identify (Zhang and Zhou, 2004: 34). So, the task of Clustering is thus to assign the properties of a feature unclassified record a certain number of clusters (ibid.).

Regression:
The goal in regression analysis is similar to the goal of the classification technique above. The difference is only that in regression no classes are formed. According to DMG this function is used to determine the relationship between the dependent variable and one or more independent variable. (Lemon *et al.*, 2003: 173). Common DM tools for Regression are linear regression and logistic regression (Ngai, Xiu and Chau, 2009: 2595).

Prediction:
Prediction is also similar to classification. The difference is, that in prediction the exception applies, the results lie in the future (Ngai *et al.*, 2011: 562). For example, one possible question of prediction analysis would be: "How would be develop the dollar exchange rate in the future?".
Neural networks and logistic model prediction are the most commonly used technique in prediction analysis (ibid.).

Visualization:
Visualization refers to presentation of data mining results so that the users can follow a complex view in the data as visual objects in dimensions and colors (Shaw et. al, 2001: 127-137). So, it is easier for the users to understand the complicated data in clear patterns and use it. "Visualization helps business and data analysts to quickly and intuitively discover interesting patterns and effectively communicate these insights to other business and data analysts, as well as, decision makers (Soukup, 2002: 5-6)."

4.3 Text Mining

The basis for all reporting, planning, analysis and balanced scorecard applications for decisions support in companies are the data warehouses, which receive their data from various operational and external data and are structured in them (Chaudhuri, Dayal and Narasayya, 2011: 90). The difference between structured, semi-structured and unstructured data has already been explained in chapter 4.1 "Big Data".

Due to the immense advances in hardware and software, the use of mobile devices and the inclusion of internet, more semi-structured (e.g. HTML files and XML's) and unstructured data such as text documents, emails, forum contributions, comments in social networks and free text input in forms, but also audios, videos and pictures. By the development of communication technologies, the simple input of the data is made possible, thus forms a huge repository.

For further understanding, the distinction between Data Mining (DM) and Text Mining (TM) is important. Theoretically, TM and DM have a common aim - exploiting information for knowledge discovery - but in practise, both technique are used separately. While DM is a process based on algorithms for analysing and extracting useful information from data, TM is responsible for transforming weak and unstructured textual data into a structured form and extract meaningful information and knowledge (Gharehchopogh and Khalifelu, 2011: 2; Hashimi, Hafez and Mathkour, 2015: 1). Most of the data that has been on the computer for years i.e. in big companies is so large, that a human cannot read and analyse it manually, so TM techniques are used to deal with such data (Hashimi, Hafez and Mathkour, 2015: 1). After the data is in a structured form, DM techniques can be applied to analyse the data.

Miner (2012: 31) divides TM into seven different practise areas and presents them in a figure, see below.

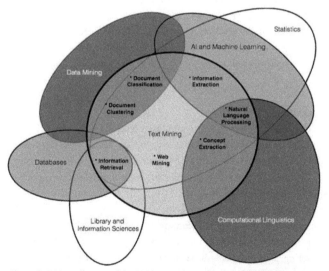

Figure 7: A Venn diagram of the TM intersection with other fields (Miner, 2012: 32)

In the figure 7, there is a distinction made between the practise areas of Information Retrieval, Document Clustering, Document Classification, Information Extraction, Natural Language

Processing, Concept Extraction and Web Mining. At the same time, the adjoining fields of research are Library and Information Science, Databases, Data Mining, Artificial Intelligence and Machine Learning, Statistics and Computer Linguistics, as well as their overlaps or touches with the individual areas. The practice areas of Text Mining are explained in more detail in the following subchapter.

4.3.1 Practise areas of Text Mining

Information Retrieval (IR)

The main task of Information Retrieval (IR) is not to analyse the data, but to index, search and retrieve documents from large text databases with keyword queries (Miner *et al.*, 2012: 36). At the present time, IR systems are used in almost every application. For example, the powerful Internet search engine Google counts on this technology, but other applications e.g. E-Mail and text editors also use IR systems by providing the user the ability to receive response through keyword queries. In summary, the goal of IR "…is to connect the right information with the right users at the right time…" (Aggarwal and Zhai, 2012: 2).

Information Extraction

Information Extraction (IE) is one of the more mature fields in text mining with the aim of constructing structured data from unstructured text (Miner *et al.*, 2012: 37). With this technique, meaningful information can be extracted from large amount of text (Talib *et al.*, 2016: 415). However, this cannot be done without great effort. Extracting data from large amount of text is not easy and requires special algorithms and softwares (Miner *et al.*, 2012: 37). "IE systems are used to extract specific attributes and entities from the document and establish their relationship. The extracted corpus is stored in the database for further processing." (Talib *et al.*, 2016: 415).

Document Clustering

According to Miner (2012: 959), clustering or cluster analysis is the oldest technology of text mining and was used by the military to document recovery systems during World War II. Today, clustering of documents is algorithms of DM used to group similar documents into clusters (ibid.: 36). The goal of clustering is to classify text documents into groups by applying different clustering algorithms (Talib *et al.*, 2016: 416). Clustering is a method of unsupervised learning; no training is required, as it is the case with supervised learning. Unsupervised learning is not as powerful as supervised learning, but more versatile. In Text Mining, clustering algorithms are used to find similar documents or specific words. If documents are analysed using clustering, this process will be called Document Clustering. If words are subject of the process, they will be called **Concept Extraction** or topic modelling (Miner *et al.*, 2012: 960). These two processes can be closely interrelated: after clustering documents are performed, the clusters are often referred to the most common words. However, word clusters can be used to categorize documents so that they can be sorted per specific concepts (ibid.).

Document Classification

In classification, the goal is not the obtaining of information, but the allocation of free text documents to a category (Gaikwad, Y Patil and Patil, 2014: 44). In a categorizing process, a free text can be assigned to one or more categories (ibid.). The goal is to train classifiers based on known examples and then automatically categorize unknown examples (ibid.). Known DM classification techniques are for example Logistic Regression (LR), Decision Tree (DT) and Support Vector Machine (SVM) (ibid.). By assigning to a category, there are basically the following procedures: First, the characteristics of the documents are selected, they describe adequately the considered context. Then the documents are examined for these properties and classified into categories. There is a distinction between binary classification and multiple classification. An example of binary classification is the differentiation of credit card transactions – fraud or non-fraud. In the further course of the thesis, a structured dataset of credit card transactions is used by dividing the transactions into two categories – fraud and non-fraud which is discussed in chapter 5.

Natural Language Processing (NLP):

In contrast to the existing techniques of Text Mining, NLP does not pursue a statistical bus a linguistic approach, in order to capture the meaning of the investigated text (Miner *et al.*, 2012: 32). A simple definition of NLP is given by Kao and Poteet (2007: 1):
"Natural language processing (NLP), is the attempt to extract a fuller meaning representation from free text. This can be put roughly as figuring out who did what to whom, when, where, how and why. "
To cope with this task, more complex algorithms (such as: neural networks) must be used to achieve acceptable results. In the field of Text Mining, NLP technique is viewed as a power-ful tool for such a problem (Miner *et al.*, 2012: 37). The requirement for NLP is the basic idea that any form of language spoken or written must be recognized first. „Natural Languages (NL) have lot of complexities as a text extracted from different sources don't have identical words or abbreviation" (Talib et al., 2016: 416). It is important that not only a word but also its connection with other words, complete sentences or facts is also identified. For the auto-matic processing and analysis of unstructured information, various tools are assigned to the NLP technique, such as the Named Entity Recognition (NER) and Part-of-Speech Tagging (Kao and Poteet, 2007: 1; Talib *et al.*, 2016: 416). In the case of NER, atomic texts are local-ized and classified into predefined categories, such as names of persons, places or firms (Pfeifer, 2014: 22). POS-Tagging is the assignment of words and punctuation marks of a text to word types (ibid.: 25).

Web Mining:

The last technique which is used by Miner (2012: 32) in the practice area of Text Mining is Web Mining (WM). "WM is defined as automatic crawling and extraction of relevant infor-mation from the artefacts, activities, and hidden patterns found in WWW" (Rashid Al-Azmi, 2013: 2). Although WM appears together with mentioned text mining techniques by Miner, it is a own practice area because of its unique structure and enormous volume of data on the Internet (Miner *et al.*, 2012: 37). Through the spread of the Internet, WM plays a very important role in our life. In many companies, this technique is used to monitor the online behaviour of the user (Rashid Al-Azmi, 2013: 2). Compared to search engines, Web Mining agents are more intelligent, since they can, for example, forward or recommend a user to a competition website (ibid.). The use of WM technology is mainly used to search for hyperlinks, cookies and patterns (ibid.). With the knowledge gathered, companies can make customer relationships better and build potential buyers with exclusive offers.

4.3.2 Example of feature extraction from unstructured data

As already mentioned in the previous chapters, around 80 % of the data is unstructured. The aim of this chapter is to show, how to bring such data in a structured form to apply them to machine learning algorithm.

Therefore, two self-generated emails are used in this thesis (see figure 7 and 8). The first email is a spam email and the second one is legitimate. With the first email, the fraudster is trying to do a phishing attack on the victim. The second email serves as an information for the online account holder for his own security.

Subject: Please update your Bank Account!!

Dear Customer,

you have not used your online bank account for a long time. Therefore, it will be deactivated automatically within 3 days. If you do not want the deactivation, please click the following link and login to update your information.

www.sp██████████.com

Best Regards
Your Online Banking Team

Figure 8: Example of a fraudulent e-mail

Subject: Two-Factor Authentication for your Online Bank Account

Dear Max Mustermann,

we always strive to increase the security of our customers. For this, you have the option to use a two-factor authentication for your access. You will find further information on the homepage of your online bank account after logging in as well as instructions for setting up two-factor authentication.

If you have further questions, please contact your local consultant.

Best Regards
Sandra Herrmann

Figure 9: Example of a legitimate e-mail

The process which is needed to transform unstructured text document, in this case emails, can be seen in figure 8 and 9. The first step in text document classification is data pre-processing. This is the first "process of extracting hidden or useful information from large dataset or document" (Undhad and Bhalodiya, 2017: 2043). The individual steps are described in more detail below:

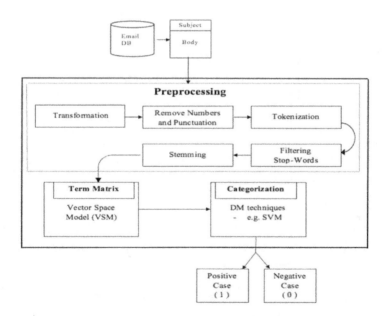

Figure 10: Text classification procedure

Transformation:
In the case of transformation (also known as normalization), which is the first step in pre-processing (see figure 10), all characters in the text file, or here in an email are converted into lowercase (Halim *et al.*, 2013: 499).

Remove Numbers and Punctuation:
In this step, all punctuation as well as numbers are removed from the email. It may happen, for example, that the words are separated by punctuation in a spam email. This has a bad influence on machine learning. Punctuation can be interpreted by machine learning differently or incorrectly (Bouchachia, 2014: 42).

Tokenization:
The task of the tokenize operator is to split the text into tokens, so that all terms are listed separately in individual tokens (Halim *et al.*, 2013: 499; Qamar, 2016: 47).

Filtering Stop-words:
In this step, the stop-words are removed from the email. Stop-words are common words that appear in every document but have no meaning. Therefore, words such as (e.g. "the", "is", "a", "and", "that") are useless as index terms (Undhad and Bhalodiya, 2017: 2044). In this thesis, the stop-word list is used from Onix Text Retrieval Toolkit[5].

Stemming:
Stemming is a process of information retrieval and the procedure to convert various forms of the same word into a single word (ibid.). Through the use of stemming algorithms, the prefixes, suffixes and unsuitable pluralizations are recognized and eliminated (Basari *et al.*, 2013: 456).

After data pre-processing step, the e-mails are in the following format.

"subject" "please" "update" "bank" "account"

"dear" "custom"

"online" "bank" "account" "long" "time" "deactivat" "automatic" "day" "deactivat" "click" "link" "log" "update" "information"

"online" "bank" "team"

Figure 11: Fraudulent e-mail after data pre-processing

---

[5] Stop-word List from Onix Text Retrieval Toolkit available at:
http://www.lextek.com/manuals/onix/stopwords2.html

"subject" "two" "factor" "authenticat" "online" "bank" "account"

"dear" "max" "mustermann"

"strive" "increase" "security" "custom" "option" "two" "factor" "authenticat" "access" "find" "further" "information" "homepage" "online" "account" "log" "in-
struction" "set" "two" "factor" "authenticat".

"further" "question" "contact" "local" "consult"

"Sandra" "herrmann"

Figure 12: Legitimate e-mail after data pre-processing

The next step, after processing the data is to create a term matrix (see figure 11). The term
matrix is used to convert the documents into numerical values to measure them subsequently
(Aggarwal and Zhai, 2012: 135-139; Yaram, 2016: 2). Vector Space Model (VSM), introduced by Salton et. at (1975: 613-620), is a technique which is used in many applications for
information – retrieval, filter and indexing (Halim *et al.*, 2013: 497). It is also widely used for
unstructured and semi-structured documents like HTML and XML (Largeron, Moulin and
Géry, 2011: 926). With help of these, the documents can be converted from terms into numerical values (Halim *et al.*, 2013: 496).

To represent document words after data processing, VSM is used to represent documents as
vectors of words (Undhad and Bhalodiya, 2017: 2044). In this approach, information or say
terms are represented in a high-dimensional metric vector space and every word is assigned to
a dimension (Vishal Gupta, 2009: 63). The column contains the number of documents D_n and
the rows represent the terms (frequency) from vocabulary (Sabbah *et al.*, 2017: 194). In this
case, the vocabulary consists of terms, which are present in the e-mail after data processing
(see figure 11 and 12). If a term appears in an email, its value is non-zero.

In many literatures (Vishal Gupta, 2009: 64; Basari *et al.*, 2013: 456; Halim *et al.*, 2013: 497;
Undhad and Bhalodiya, 2017: 2044) Term Frequency (TF) and Term Frequency – Inverse
Document Frequency (TF-IDF) are used in vector space model as a weighting scheme. TF is
the measure of how many times terms are present in a document D. An example, with first six
terms from email 1 and 2 (see figure 11 and 12) is shown in table 1 below:

		Count tf_i	
	Terms	D_1	D_2
1	subject	1	1
2	update	2	0
3	dear	1	1
4	custom	1	1

5	online	2	1
6	account	2	2
n	...	...	...

Table 1: Vector Space – Count TF

The resulting vector in table above shows 1 occurrences of the term "subject" in both documents, 2 occurrences of the term "update" in document D_1 and 0 occurrences in document D_2 and so on.

After representing term frequencies in a vector space, the vector can be converted in a document matrix M_{tf}. An example:

$$M_{tf} = \begin{bmatrix} 1 & 2 & 1 & 1 & 2 & 2 \\ 1 & 0 & 1 & 1 & 1 & 2 \end{bmatrix}$$

A problem with TF is that the frequently used terms are scaled upwards and the rarely occurring terms are scaled down, which are more informative. The basic intuition is "...that a query term which occurs in many documents is not a good discriminator, and should be given less weight than one which occurs in few documents..." (Robertson, 2004: 503). To solve this kind of problem, Term Frequency – Inverse Document Frequency (TF-IDF) comes into play (ibid.).

IDF is defined as (Sabbah *et al.*, 2017: 196):

$$idf_{(t)} = log \frac{|D|}{1 + |\{d : t \in d\}|}$$

The document space is defined as D where $N = |D|$ is the total number of documents in vector space and $|\{d : t \in d\}|$ is the number of documents where the term t appears, at least one time (Largeron, Moulin and Géry, 2011: 926). To avoid division by zero, 1 was added in the denominator (Sabbah *et al.*, 2017: 196). With this equation, the frequently occurring terms are scaled down and rare occurrences are scaled up (ibid.).

TF-IDF is defined as (ibid.):

$$tf - idf_{(t)} = tf(t, d) \; x \; idf(t)$$

To keep the calculations manageable, the e-mails of figure 9 and 10 will not be used. Instead, a random matrix with four anonymous terms t (features: W, X, Y, Z) and two documents D is created. The process with the emails is the same:

$$M_{tf} = \begin{bmatrix} 1 & 2 & 1 & 0 \\ 1 & 0 & 2 & 0 \end{bmatrix}$$

For the four features the IDF can be calculated as follows (ibid.):

$$idf\,(t1) = \log\frac{|D|}{1 + |\{d : t \in d\}|} = \log\frac{2}{3} = -0.4055$$

$$idf\,(t2) = \log\frac{|D|}{1 + |\{d : t \in d\}|} = \log\frac{2}{3} = -0.4055$$

$$idf\,(t3) = \log\frac{|D|}{1 + |\{d : t \in d\}|} = \log\frac{2}{4} = -0.6931$$

$$idf\,(t4) = \log\frac{|D|}{1 + |\{d : t \in d\}|} = \log\frac{2}{1} = 0.6931$$

After calculating the IDF weight, it can be presented in a vector as follows:

$$idf^{\rightarrow} = (-0.4055, -0.4055, -0.6931, 0.6931)$$

With the matrix of term frequency M_{tf} and the vector representing the idf for each feature of the matrix, the calculation of TF-IDF weights can be done. Before this, a square diagonal matrix[6] M_{idf} is created to make the calculation clearer. Thereafter, the matrix M_{tf} is multiplied by the matrix M_{idf} as follows:

$$M_{idf} = \begin{bmatrix} -0.4055 & 0 & 0 & 0 \\ 0 & -0.4055 & 0 & 0 \\ 0 & 0 & -0.6931 & 0 \\ 0 & 0 & 0 & 0.6931 \end{bmatrix}$$

Calculation method: Multiplying each IDF value to its corresponding feature.

$$M_{tf-idf} = \begin{bmatrix} 1 & 2 & 1 & 0 \\ 1 & 0 & 2 & 0 \end{bmatrix} \times \begin{bmatrix} -0.4055 & 0 & 0 & 0 \\ 0 & -0.4055 & 0 & 0 \\ 0 & 0 & -0.6931 & 0 \\ 0 & 0 & 0 & 0.6931 \end{bmatrix}$$

$$M_{tf-idf} = \begin{bmatrix} tf_{(t1,d1)} \times idf_{(t1)} & tf_{(t2,d1)} \times idf_{(t2)} & tf_{(t3,d1)} \times idf_{(t3)} & tf_{(t4,d1)} \times idf_{(t4)} \\ tf_{(t1,d2)} \times idf_{(t1)} & tf_{(t2,d2)} \times idf_{(t2)} & tf_{(t1,d2)} \times idf_{(t3)} & tf_{(t4,d2)} \times idf_{(t4)} \end{bmatrix}$$

---

[6] Diagonal matrix: https://en.wikipedia.org/wiki/Diagonal_matrix

$$M_{tf-idf} = \begin{bmatrix} -0.4055 & -0.811 & -0.6931 & 0 \\ -0.4055 & 0 & -1.3862 & 0 \end{bmatrix}$$

In this chapter, TM was used to show how unstructured data can be converted in a structured form to apply the data on machine learning algorithms. In the example, the procedure was shown on an e-mail database, but the use of TM method on other unstructured textual data is the same.

A detailed literature review by Bhattacharya and West (2016) on financial fraud shows, that many authors use text mining approaches to detect fraud in financial statement fraud. Bhattacharya and West define text mining method as: "Highly useful for fraud types with large amounts of textual data, such as financial statement fraud." (West and Bhattacharya, 2016: 52).

After the data has passed through the pre-processing step, the data for the feature extraction is available. Then these can be transferred to a structured form with the use of term matrix and term weighting to apply these data subsequently on predictive data mining techniques. With DM techniques, a positive case or a negative case can be predicted. A case can be positive if for example a fraud in the dataset exists, otherwise the case is negative. More about use of several DM techniques a study on credit card fraud detection in the following chapter is made.

4.4   Context of Data Mining and Text Mining in White-Collar Crime

The conclusion from this chapter is, that DM and TM plays a major role in white-collar crime to detect fraud in data. The structured data can be found most in a relational database. The mentioned types of white-collar crime presented in chapter 3 are examples of such types of fraud that are available in a relational database and can be directly applied to various predictive data mining techniques to detect fraud. However, as already mentioned in chapter 4.1, a large number of data, about 80 percent, exists in unstructured format (Gharehchopogh and Khalifelu, 2011: 1; Gupta and Gill, 2012: 73; Talib et al., 2016: 414). TM is brought in use to extract meaningful information from the textual data and to convert these data in structured form. Therefore, one can say, that TM plays an important role in white-collar crime as much as DM. TM is responsible for transforming weak and unstructured textual data into a structured form and extract meaningful information and knowledge (Gharehchopogh and Khalifelu, 2011: 2; Hashimi, Hafez and Mathkour, 2015: 1).

In a journal (Gupta and Gill, 2012: 189-191) the authors mention the importance of TM and DM in financial statement fraud because it "...is a major concern for most of the organization worldwide" (ibid.: 191). The released financial statements of companies consist of unstructured textual information in the "… form of auditor's comments and disclosure as footnotes along with financial ratios" (ibid.: 189). The authors define such indicators as qualitative information for fraudulent financial reporting (ibid.). To detect fraudulent financial reports, the informal text must first be transformed in structured form before predictive data mining techniques such as classification or clustering can be used (ibid.).

5   A case study on Credit Card Fraud Detection

5.1   Overview

In this chapter, several DM techniques are used to detect fraud in the credit card dataset. The credit card dataset is obtainable from Kaggle.com[7] and contains a subset of European credit card transactions, made in September 2013 over a period of two days.   The dataset has been collected and analysed during a research collaboration of Worldline and the Machine Learning Group (http://mlg.ulb.ac.be) of ULB (Université Libre de Bruxelles) on Big Data Mining and Fraud Detection.

To deal with these data, Jupyter Notebook[8] was used. Jupyter notebook provide a powerful tool for the analysis of data and includes the programming language Julia, Python and R.

5.2   Data Exploration

Before the use of several DM techniques to discover fraud, it is important to look first at the data to get an overview of the form in which the data are available. To load the data into Jupyter Notebook the panda (python data analysis library) method *read_csv* is used and with the *.head()* function the data is present in a table.

```
1. import pandas as pd #load library
2. data = pd.read_csv("file:///Users/Desktop/Dataset/CreditCardData/creditcard
   .csv",header = 0)
3. data.head()
4. data.shape
```

	Time	V1	V2	V3	V4	V5	V6	V7	V8	V9
0	0.0	-1.359807	-0.072781	2.536347	1.378155	-0.338321	0.462388	0.239599	0.098698	0.363787
1	0.0	1.191857	0.266151	0.166480	0.448154	0.060018	-0.082361	-0.078803	0.085102	-0.255425
2	1.0	-1.358354	-1.340163	1.773209	0.379780	-0.503198	1.800499	0.791461	0.247676	-1.514654
3	1.0	-0.966272	-0.185226	1.792993	-0.863291	-0.010309	1.247203	0.237609	0.377436	-1.387024
4	2.0	-1.158233	0.877737	1.548718	0.403034	-0.407193	0.095921	0.592941	-0.270533	0.817739

---

[7] Credit card fraud dataset available at: https://www.kaggle.com/dalpozz/creditcardfraud
[8] Official Website of Jupyter: http://jupyter.org/

V21	V22	V23	V24	V25	V26	V27	V28	Amount	Class
-0.018307	0.277838	-0.110474	0.066928	0.128539	-0.189115	0.133558	-0.021053	149.62	0
-0.225775	-0.638672	0.101288	-0.339846	0.167170	0.125895	-0.008983	0.014724	2.69	0
0.247998	0.771679	0.909412	-0.689281	-0.327642	-0.139097	-0.055353	-0.059752	378.66	0
-0.108300	0.005274	-0.190321	-1.175575	0.647376	-0.221929	0.062723	0.061458	123.50	0
-0.009431	0.798278	-0.137458	0.141267	-0.206010	0.502292	0.219422	0.215153	69.99	0

Figure 13: Import of credit card data in Juypter notebook

Only the first 5 rows are displayed in the figure 13. The dataset contains only numerical input variables. Using the *.shape* function the number of rows and columns can be displayed.

Output:
```
(284807, 31)
```

The dataset has 284807 rows and 31 columns with the features Times, V1 to V28 (anonymized), Amount and Class. The features from V1 to V28 are anonymized and normalised obtained from a set of original features using Principal Component Analysis (PCA) (Boys, 2016). PCA is a standard method for feature normalisation. The features Time, Amount and Class are not transformed with PCA. The last feature is named Class and can contain either 0 or 1. Here, 0 means that it is a normal transaction and 1 indicates a fraudulent transaction.

In the next step an analysis is made to see how many normal transactions and how many fraudulent transactions are contained in the data set.

```
5.  non_frauds = len(data[data["Class"]==0])
6.  frauds = len(data[data["Class"]==1])
7.  total = non_frauds+frauds
8.  print "Normal (non-fraud) transaction:", non_frauds
9.  print "Fraud transaction:", frauds
10. print "Total transaction:", total
11.
12. f_percent = (frauds / float(total)) * 100
13. print "Percentage of fraudlument transaction: {:.2f}%".format(f_percent)
14.
15. n_percent = (non_frauds / float(total)) * 100
16. print "Percentage of normal (non-frauds) transaction:  {:.2f}%".format(n_percent)
17.
18. # draw matplot
19. sns.countplot("Class",data=data)
```

Output:
```
Normal (non-fraud) transaction: 284315
Fraud transaction: 492
Total transaction: 284807
Percentage of fraudulent transaction: 0.17%
Percentage of normal (non-fraud) transaction: 99.83%
```

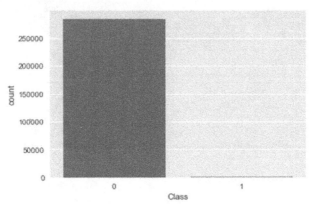

Figure 14: Imbalanced class in credit card dataset

The output and the figure 14 shows that only 0.17 % (492 transactions out of 284807 transactions) are fraudulent. This means, there is a highly imbalanced dataset, which must take into consideration for the further investigation.

With the feature "Amount" in the dataset, a visualization of fraudulent and non-fraudulent transactions can be displayed in a plot. Since very few fraudulent transactions appear in the record, it would be interesting to know how big the damage for such fraudulent transactions is.

```
20. plt.figure(figsize=(20,8))
21. plt.ylim(0,3000)
22. plt.plot(data['Amount'])
23. plt.plot(data[data['Class']==1]['Amount'],'ro')
24. plt.show()
```

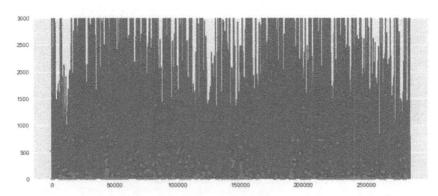

Figure 15: Plot of normal and fraudulent transaction

In the plot (figure15) non-fraud transactions are marked blue and fraudulent transactions are marked red. The most fraudulent transactions are small amounts, less than 100 and the largest amount in fraudulent transaction is near 2300.

As already mentioned, the balance of normal and fraudulent transactions plays an important role in the dataset, this may not be ignored in the further analysis. In the next step, the data remain unbalanced and different techniques will be used to detect fraud and make a prediction.

```
25. X = data.ix[:, data.columns != 'Class']
26. y = data.ix[:, data.columns == 'Class']
```

The predictor variable is assigned to object X and the target variable to object Y. More about target and prediction classes see in Chapter 6.3 (Confusion Matrix Terminology) below.

It can be seen in figure 13, that the transactions are anonymized from column V1 to V28. Therefore, it is not known which scale is used for which feature in the dataset. If the scales are different for different features, this can have a knock-on-effect in the ability to learn. To be on the safe side with such data, normalization is a good technique for that. "Data normalization is the process of rescaling one or more attributes to the range of 0 to 1. This means that the largest value for each attribute is 1 and the smallest value is 0." (Browniee, 2016).

```
27. from sklearn.preprocessing import StandardScaler
28. X["Normalized Amount"] = StandardScaler().fit_transform(X["Amount"].values.reshape(-
    1, 1))
29. X = X.drop(["Time", "Amount"], axis=1)
30. X.head()
```

Output:

V20	V21	V22	V23	V24	V25	V26	V27	V28	Normalized Amount
0.251412	-0.018307	0.277838	-0.110474	0.066928	0.128539	-0.189115	0.133558	-0.021053	0.244964
-0.069083	-0.225775	-0.638672	0.101288	-0.339846	0.167170	0.125895	-0.008983	0.014724	-0.342475
0.524980	0.247998	0.771679	0.909412	-0.689281	-0.327642	-0.139097	-0.055353	-0.059752	1.160686
-0.208038	-0.108300	0.005274	-0.190321	-1.175575	0.647376	-0.221929	0.062723	0.061458	0.140534
0.408542	-0.009431	0.798278	-0.137458	0.141267	-0.206010	0.502292	0.219422	0.215153	-0.073403

Figure 16: Credit card data after normalization

5.3   Confusion Matrix Terminology

To evaluate a classifier, Classification Report is used, which has the following performance measures: Recall, Precision, F1- Score and Accuracy. Furthermore, confusion matrix is used in this classification analysis to evaluate a classifier. A confusion matrix is a table or plot that is often used to describe the performance of a classification model (Markham, 2014). The confusion matrix consists 2 target classes and 2 predicted classes.

		Predicted Class	
		Predicted = YES	Predicted = NO
Target Class	Target = YES	True Positive (TP)	False Negative (FN)
	Target = NO	False Positive (FP)	True Negative (TN)

Table 2: Confusion Matrix

In the table 2, two green and two red table cells can be seen. True positives and true negatives are the observations which are predicted correctly. The goal is to minimize false positives and false negatives, because these are not properly predicted.

Positive:
Indicates that an observation is positive. For example: is a fraud (Albon, 2016).

Negative:
Indicates that an observation is negative. For example: is not a fraud (Albon, 2016).

True Positive (TP):
An observation which is positive, is predicted as positive (Akosa, 2017: 3). It means, the value of target class is YES and the value of the predicted class is also YES (Joshi, 2016). For example: A fraud is predicted as Fraud.

False Negative (FN):
An observation which is positive, is predicted as negative (Akosa, 2017: 3). The target class in this case is YES and predicted class is NO (Joshi, 2016). For example: A fraud is predicted as non-fraud.

False Positive (FP):
An observation which is negative, is predicted as positive (Akosa, 2017: 3).The target class in this case is NO and the predicted class is YES (Joshi, 2016). For example: A non-fraud is predicted as fraud.

True Negative (TN):

An observation which is negative, is predicted correctly as negative (Akosa, 2017: 3). In this case both class have the value NO (Joshi, 2016). For example: A non-fraud is predicted as non-fraud.

Recall:

Recall is also called Sensitivity and is the ration of correctly predicted positive observations to all observations in target class 'YES' (Powers, 2011: 38 & Vafeiadis *et al.*, 2015: 3).

$$recall = \frac{True\ Positive}{True\ Positive + False\ Negative}$$

Precision:

Precision is also called Confidence in DM and is the ratio of correctly predicted positive observations to the total predicted positive observations (Powers, 2011: 38 & Vafeiadis *et al.*, 2015: 3).

$$precision = \frac{True\ Positive}{True\ Positive + False\ Positive}$$

F1-Score:

"F1-Score is defined as the harmonic mean of precision and recall" (Weiss et.al., 2010: 70). In other words, F-measure has a parameter that sets the tradeoff between precision and recall. The standard F-measure is F1, which gives equal importance to recall and precision.

$$F1 = 2 * \frac{precision * recall}{precision + recall}$$

Accuracy:

"Accuracy is the most intuitive performance measure and it is simply a ratio of correctly predicted observation to the total observations" (Joshi, 2016). The result of Accuracy says how good the model is.

$$Accuracy = \frac{True\ Positive + True\ Negative}{True\ Positive + False\ Negative + False\ Positive + True\ Negative}$$

5.4   Algorithms and Techniques

5.4.1   Literature review on Data Mining Techniques

For the selection of DM techniques, a literature review is necessary. Since there exist already many literature reviews on fraud detection, these will be analysed and summarized for the selection of DM techniques for the credit card dataset. In addition, it is assumed, that DM techniques are selected which can be used in other fraud datasets. The aim is to make a connection to the chapter 3 "Types of White-Collar Crimes". The investigation assumes, that the mentioned fraud types are in a structured form, such as the credit card dataset. If the data is in an unstructured form, first it must be transformed in a structured form using the text mining approach, which was demonstrated in Chapter 4.3 using an example of e-mail database.

To select the literature the following procedure was used: Only journals and articles from free available online databases were used. The search was restricted and used only the following databases: Google Scholar, ScienceDirect and SpringerLink. To find the most relevant literatures the search was also restricted to Abstract, Title and Keywords. Following keywords were used for the search: *Data Mining and Financial Fraud Detection*. For this, the operator (AND) has been used in the advanced searches of each databases. Also, only those journals and articles that had been published between 2011 and 2017 were selected. To limit the further search, it was considered that only literatures which use and compares at least three DM techniques are selected. Furthermore, several types of fraud should be treated in selected literatures.

The result of the literature search showed, that total 5 articles are found, which are most relevant for the further investigation.

In a comprehensive literature review by Albashrawi (2016: 553-570), a total of 65 relevant articles for financial fraud detection using data mining techniques in the period from 2004 to 2015 are examined. The review shows, that a total of 41 DM techniques were used to detect fraud in financial area (ibid.). The author found out, that more supervised learning tools were used more than unsupervised DM techniques (ibid.: 553). A classification framework was created and the financial fraud was divided into four categories: Financial Statement Fraud, Bank Fraud, Insurance Fraud and other financial related fraud (ibid.: 562). Bank fraud was sub-classified to credit card fraud, account fraud and money laundering whereas insurance fraud was sub-classified to crop fraud, automobile fraud and healthcare fraud (ibid.). For the presentation of the result, a table was prepared by Albashrawi (2016: 560) in which the DM techniques and types of fraud were listed and the number of occurrences of a DM technique was assigned to the fraud (ibid.). The result was, that Logistic Regression (LR), Neural Network (NN), Decision Trees (DT), Support Vector Machine (SVM) and Naïve Bayes (NB) are the top 5 most commonly used DM techniques for fraud detection in various fraud areas (ibid.: 560). The following table shows the occurrence, usage frequency (ibid.) and the fraud areas (ibid.: 562) of most commonly DM technique as result of the review.

DM-Method	Occurrence	Usage Frequency	Fraud Areas
Logistic Regression	13	17	Financial Statement Fraud, Credit Card Fraud, Auto Fraud, Crop Fraud, Other financial Frauds
Neural Network	14	15	Financial Statement Fraud, Credit Card Fraud, Auto Fraud, Other financial Frauds
Decision Trees	14	15	Financial Statement Fraud, Credit Card Fraud, Auto Fraud, Other financial Frauds
Support Vector Machine	9	12	Financial Statement Fraud, Credit Card Fraud, Other financial Frauds
Naïve Bayes	8	8	Credit Card Fraud, Auto Fraud, Other financial Frauds

Table 3: Top five ranked Data Mining methods by Albashrawi (2016: 560)

Another study by Lin *et al.* (2015) uses Logistic Regression (LR), Decision Tree (CART) and Artificial Neural Networks (ANN) as DM techniques to detect fraud in financial statement. The aim of the study is to investigate and evaluate all aspects of the fraud triangle (pressure/incentive, opportunity and attitude/rationalization (see chapter: 2.2) using DM techniques (ibid. 459-470). Therefore, a dataset of 129 fraud cases and 447 legitimate cases was used to test the machine learning system (ibid.).

The result showed, that all three used DM techniques are suitable for detecting financial statement fraud (ibid.: 468). ANN and DT have achieved a better classification rate (> 90%) (ibid.). LR model was somewhat weaker in comparison and achieved a correct classification rate in training data with 83.7 % and in test data with 88.5 % (ibid.).

In a journal article from Yaram (2016) an implementation of document-clustering algorithms (unsupervised learning technique) and classification algorithms (supervised learning techniques) for fraud detection was made. For the classification algorithms, the author used the following DM techniques: DT, RF and NB. For the investigation, the data are available in structured, semi-structured and unstructured format (ibid.: 1). The author used K-Means clustering as a document clustering algorithm and used the pre-processing approach (TM) to transform the unstructured data in a structured way to apply the data on the DM techniques (ibid.: 2-3). The result of the analysis was that DT and RF algorithms perform better than NB algorithm (ibid.: 6). The accuracy with DT and RF classifier was achieved with over 90 % and with NB classifier only 74.19 % (ibid).

In the literature review of Bhattacharya and West (2016) more than 50 articles (published from 2004 to 2014) were analysed in relation to financial fraud. Financial fraud was divided into 4 sub-categories: Credit Card Fraud, Insurance Fraud, Financial Statement Fraud and Securities and Commodities Fraud. The analysis has revealed, that there is a total of 13 DM techniques that are most commonly used in financial fraud area (ibid.: 51).

Neural networks can solve binary classification problems and are well established with fraud detection but require high computational power for training and operation (ibid.: 52). They can also lead to overfitting as well as at RF and DT, if the training set is not good enough (ibid.). LR model has been assigned by the authors to insurance fraud (ibid.:51). A good feature of Logistic Model is, that it is simple to implement, like DT, RF and genetic algorithm but has a lower classification performance than other DM techniques (ibid.:52). SVM is a good technique to solve non-linear classification problems but needs also high computational power (ibid.). TM is "(h)ighly useful for fraud types with large amounts of textual data, such as financial statement fraud" but "(r)euquires another classification method to perform the actual fraud detection" (ibid.). Bayesian belief network is good as SVM can solve binary classification problems but "requires strong understanding of typical and abnormal behaviour for the investigated fraud type" (ibid.).

The examined articles by Bhattacharya and West (2016) have shown, that especially in Financial Statement Fraud, the most commonly used DM techniques are such as TM, BBN, DT, NN, SVM, LR which achieve a satisfactory accuracy and sensitivity.

In an empirical study on financial risk prediction by Peng et al. (2011), 8 DM techniques on 6 financial risk datasets, were used. Australia and Germany indicate the credit card application data (German: 70 % accepted application and 30 % rejected applications, Australia: 55.5 % accepted application and 44.5 % rejected applications); USA and China provide the behavioural data of credit card holders (USA: 84 % good accounts and 16 % bad accounts, China: 91.9 % good accounts and 8.1 % bad accounts); Japan (37 bankrupt and 111 non-bankrupt firms) and Korea (65 bankrupt and 130 non-bankrupt firms) provide the bankruptcy data and India provides the insurance data with 353 abnormal and 18522 normal claims (Peng *et al.*, 2011: 2910). The 8 DM techniques used in this study are: Bayesian Network (BN), Naïve Bayes (NB), Logistic Regression (LR), K-nearest Neighbor, C4.5, RIPPER rule induction and radial basis function (RBF) network (ibid.). To evaluate the classification algorithm, the authors uses the criteria: accuracy, precision, area under the curve, true-positive rate and true-negative rate.

The results show that in Australian dataset DM techniques BN (precision: 85.96 %), NB (TN-rate: 92.17 %), SVM (TP-rate: 92.51 %) and LR model (AUC: 93.12 %) achieve the best classification result.

In the high imbalanced dataset from India, Naïve Bayes and Bayesian Network are well suited classifiers. "Naïve Bayes has the highest TP rate (0.9065), which indicates that it captured 90.65% of the abnormal records, while Bayesian Network achieves a good TN rate (0.8291)" (Peng *et al.*, 2011: 2912). In the dataset from China und USA the DM techniques NB, SVM and LR gives also a good accuracy, precision, TP and TN rate (ibid.: 2911). The result in a small dataset, like the dataset Japanese bankruptcy data, was that no classifier performs well enough and produces satisfactory result.

5.4.2 Selection of Data Mining Techniques

Based on the literature analysis, the following data mining techniques are selected for the case study. The selection is based on ease of use and noted performance advantages in the literature.

Support Vector Machine:

SVM is a supervised machine learning algorithm which can be used for classification and regression and is also very successful in fraud detection problems (Tong and Koller, 2001: 47; Chen, Shu-Ting and Shiue-Shiun, 2006: 30; Zareapoor, Seeja.K.R and Afshar Alam, 2012: 36). „The simple geometrical explanation of this approach involves determining an optimal separating plane or hyperplane that separates the two classes or clusters of data points justly and is equidistant from both of them" (Kajaree and Behera, 2017: 1306). First, SVM was defined as a linear distribution of data points, but with the introduction of kernel functions, non-linear data can also be processed, thus, complex and non-linear problems such as the detection of financial fraud can be solved by linear classification (Bhattacharyya et al., 2011: 604; Kajaree and Behera, 2017: 1306).

Random Forest:

Random Forest (RF) is an ensemble of decision trees and at the same time an ensemble learning method for classification (Pandey et al., 2017: 5 and Seeja and Zareapoor, 2014: 3). Seeja and Zareapoor (2014: 3) explain how RF works in very simple words: "The basic principle behind ensemble methods is that a group of 'weak learner' can come together to form a 'strong learner' (…) while all the decision trees taken together are a 'strong learner'. When a new object is to be classified, it is run down in each of the trees in the forest. Each tree gives a classification output or 'vote' for a class. The forest classifies the new object into the class having maximum votes." (Mahmud, Meesad and Sodsee, 2016: 2).

RF need computationally efficient because of the large number of trees, but an advantage of RF model is, that they are robust to overfitting and noise in the data (Bhattacharyya et al., 2011: 605).

Decision Tree:

DT is one of the most successful supervised learning algorithms in data mining, also known as a classification tree, and has a similar logic to the Random Forest technique (Kajaree and Behera, 2017: 1306). Decision Trees become one of the most powerful and popular approaches in DM for exploring large data to discover useful patterns (Dhanapal and Gayathiri P, 2012: 408).

„It constructs a graph or tree that employs branching technique to demonstrate every probable result of a decision. In a decision tree representation, every internal node tests a feature, each branch corresponds to outcome of the parent node and every leaf finally assigns the class label. To classify an instance, a top-down approach is applied starting at the root of the tree. For a certain feature or node, the branch concurring to the value of the data point for that attribute is considered till a leaf is reached or a label is decided" (Kajaree and Behera, 2017: 1306).

Logistic Regression:

LR technique is a widely-used technique in financial fraud detection. It is a suitable regression analysis to conduct when the dependent variable is binary (Bhattacharyya *et al.*, 2011: 604). This is a standard method for binary target variable with multiple features (Kibekbaev and Duman, 2016: 101). "Logistic regression is used to describe data and to explain the relationship between one dependent binary variable and one or more nominal, ordinal, interval or ratio-level independent variables" (ibid.).

Multi-Layer Perception (MLP-Classifier):

MLP Classifier is a popular network architecture used for classification and regression (Zanaty, 2012: 179). This classifier belongs to neural networks and "MLPs are feed forward neural networks which are typically composed of several layers of nodes with unidirectional connections, often trained by back propagation. The learning process of MLP network is based on the data samples composed of the N-dimensional input vector x and the M-dimensional desired output vector d, called destination. By processing the input vector x, the MLP produces the output signal vector y(x,w) where w is the vector of adapted weights" (ibid.).

Naïve Bayes:

Naïve-Bayes method "… is a probabilistic classifier baes on the Bayes theorem" (Humpherys, Moffitt et al. 2011). It is assumed, that a dataset is represented with a certain probability by a specified vector and that this dataset can be classified into a corresponding class with a certain probability (Kajaree and Behera, 2017; Pandey et al., 2017). "It assumes that the values of the features are independent of each other, given a class label" (Pandey et al., 2017). The presence of one feature is by no means affected by the presence of another feature (ibid.).

5.5 Sampling techniques

As for the data in the dataset, it was found that the data is in an unbalanced state (see chapter 5.2: Data Exploration). There is a minority class with fraud transaction (contains 0.17 %) and a majority class with normal (non-fraud) transactions (contains 99.83 %). To deal with such imbalanced data, different sampling techniques exist. Data Sampling is a statistical analysis method (Rouse, 2016). With these techniques, a representative subset of data can be selected, processed and analyzed (ibid.). In the following, the sampling techniques will be explained in more detail, which will also be used in the further procedure.

No Sampling:

In the case of no sampling, "(a)ll of the data points from majority and minority training sets are used" (Dubey *et al.*, 2014: 6).

Undersampling:

The simplest technique at undersampling in imbalanced dataset is the random undersampling of the majority class (More, 2016: 2). "All of the training data points from the minority class are used. Instances are randomly removed from the majority training set till the desired balanced is achieved" (Dubey *et al.*, 2014: 6). A probable disadvantage is that some important information can be lost during the undersampling process (ibid.).

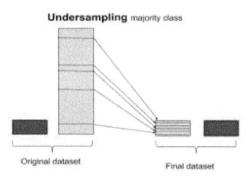

Figure 17: Undersampling of majority class (Fawcett, 2016)

In the figure 17, the dataset is displayed in a red and a light blue diagram. In the dataset of credit card, the red column of the diagram represents the fraud class and the light blue diagram shows the normal class. In the second approach, random undersampling technique will be used. The non-fraud transactions class 0 (majority class) will be undersample to fraudulent transactions class 1 (minority class).

Oversampling:

In the case of oversampling, all minority and majority training sets are used as well as in the case of no-sampling (Dubey *et al.*, 2014: 6). The difference is, that data from minority training set are duplicated till the desired balance is achieved (ibid.). The problem with the oversampling technique is that the result can lead to overfitting, since the information from the minority class is simply generated, which cannot be relevant to the learning (More, n.d.: 5 & Dal Pozzolo, 2015: 47).

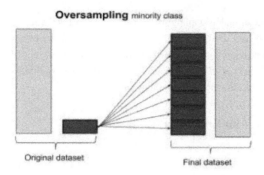

Figure 18: Oversampling of minority class (Fawcett, 2016)

In the third approach, oversampling technique will be used and the fraud data (minority class) will be oversample to non-fraud data (majority class).

SMOTE:

The acronym SMOTE stands for "Synthetic Minority Oversampling Technique" and is a another technique to oversample the data. (Dubey *et al.*, 2014: 6). In this case, SMOTE technique

"… oversample the minority class by generating synthetic examples in the neighborhood of observed ones. The idea is to form new minority examples by interpolating between samples of the same class. This has the effect of creating clusters around each minority observation. By creating synthetic observations the classifier builds larger decision regions that contain nearby instances from the minority class." (Dal Pozzolo, 2015: 37).

In many literatures the SMOTE technique is preferred and used instead of the random oversampling technique (Dal Pozzolo, 2015: 37 & Zhuoyuan et. al., 2015: 2).

In the fourth approach, the SMOTE Oversampling technique will be used and compared with other sampling and especially with random oversampling technique.

5.6   Train and Test Set

After the normalization process, the *train_test_split* function will be used to split the data into test and train set. In many literatures and examples, the data is divided into train and test set and retain 30% to test the model. Since no clear evidence exists which method of splitting is best, the following combinations are tried on the imbalanced data: 20/80, 25/75, 30/70. The results are shown in the table 4 below.

	Precision	Recall	F1-Score	Accuracy	Test / Train
LR	0.88	0.63	0.74	0.9992	20/80

LR	0.88	0.67	0.76	0.9992	25/75
LR	0.88	0.62	0.72	0.9992	30/70
RF	0.92	0.75	0.83	0.9995	20/80
RF	0.94	0.72	0.82	0.9995	25/75
RF	0.96	0.75	0.84	0.9995	30/70
SVM	0.92	0.66	0.77	0.9993	20/80
SVM	0.93	0.65	0.76	0.9993	25/75
SVM	0.95	0.63	0.75	0.9993	30/70
DT	0.78	0.77	0.78	0.9992	20/80
DT	0.79	0.78	0.78	0.9992	25/75
DT	0.79	0.73	0.77	0.9992	30/70

Table 4: Results for selection of the best split

F1-Score is the harmonic mean of precision and recall (Weiss et.al., 2010: 70), therefore, only the results of precision and recall are compared in LR, RF, SVM and DT.

In LR, the result of precision in all three splitting cases is the same but the result for recall are different. With 25/75 split, recall has the best result in comparison to the other. At RF, the decision is somewhat more difficult. In the three splitting cases, the Precision is better the larger the test set is. Recall is equal at 20/80 and 30/70 split and at 25/75 split, recall loses 3%. With SVM, the best result is between 20/80 and 30/70 split. In 20/80 split, the recall is good, but precision bad. In 30/70 division, the precision is good, whereas the recall is bad. At DT result it is just as easy to recognize as with the LR result. The result of precision is almost same in all cases, but the best achieved result in the recall column is with 25/75 split. For the further investigation, the 25/75 split will be used.

5.7 Imbalanced Data

In the first approach, no sampling technique will be used and the data is unbalanced in the class. Before using DM techniques LR, RF, SVM, DT, NN and NB the data is split into train and test set (see chapter 5.6: Train and Test Set).

Output:
```
Predictor train set:   (213605, 29)
Predictor test set:    (71202, 29)
Target train set:      (213605,)
Target test set:       (71202,)
```

25% (71202 out of 284807) is retained to test the model and 75% for train set. Now the mentioned DM techniques can be used. In the first step, an object of the model is created, then the model is trained on the train set and in the last step a prediction can be made on the test set.

Here is an example on the model LR:

```
1. # create a LR object.
2. lr = LogisticRegression()
3. # train the model on training set
4. lr.fit(X_train, y_train)
5. # make predictions based on test set
6. lrpred = lr.predict(X_test)
```

5.7.1 Results on imbalanced Data

Table 5 shows the six machine learning techniques used with their results of classification report. The first column shows the model used for making prediction. The second column contain the results of precision, also called confidence in DM and is the ration of correctly predicted positive conversations to the total predicted positive observations. The next column is for Recall and is the fraction of correctly predicted positive observations to all observations in the positive target class. This one is followed by the column F1-Score which is defined as the harmonic mean of precision and recall. The result of accuracy indicates how close a measured value is to the actual true value. The sampling type is listed in the next column. In this approach, no sampling technique was used. Another interesting aspect will be the duration on differently weighted data. Therefore, the time in seconds is represented in the last column. In this way, all future results of different approaches are presented in one table.

	Precision	Recall	F1-Score	Accuracy	Sampling type	Time in sec
Logistic Regression	0.88	0.67	0.76	0.9992	Imbalanced Data	2
RF-Classifier	0.92	0.74	0.82	0.9995	Imbalanced Data	25
SVM (Support Vector Classifier)	0.93	0.65	0.76	0.9993	Imbalanced Data	176
DT (Decision Tree Classifier)	0.76	0.75	0.75	0.9992	Imbalanced Data	17
Neural Network (MLP Classifier)	0.91	0.77	0.83	0.9995	Imbalanced Data	20
Naïve Bayes (GaussianNB)	0.06	0.83	0.12	0.9784	Imbalanced Data	3

Table 5: Results on imbalanced data using DM techniques

A view of the column accuracy shows, that for all used predictive models except NB the value of accuracy is higher than 99 %. A high precision on imbalanced data is achieved with RF Classifier (92 %) and SVM (93 %). It means, that a transaction which is classified as a fraud is truly a fraud. The highest recall is achieved with RF Classifier. 74 % is the probability that a true fraud in the test data is recognized by the classifier. NB Classifier is the worst choice on imbalanced dataset in this case. Although, recall is as good as RF Classifier, the precision is very low with only 6 %. It shows, that SVM has also a good precision, like RF Classifier. However, the recall here is bad here and this model needs the most time to make a prediction. A decision before other approaches come into play is that on imbalanced dataset, the RF Classifier and NN with 99.95 % accuracy are best suited.

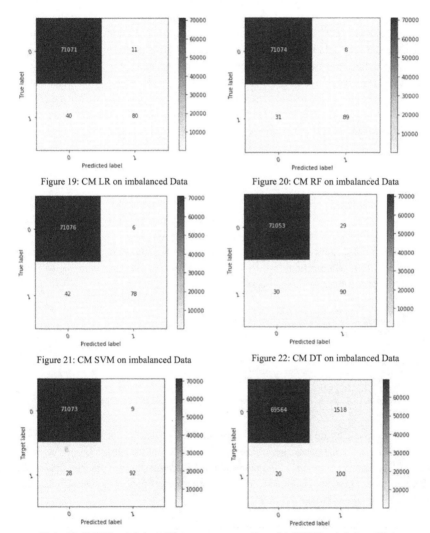

Figure 19: CM LR on imbalanced Data   Figure 20: CM RF on imbalanced Data

Figure 21: CM SVM on imbalanced Data   Figure 22: CM DT on imbalanced Data

Figure 23: CM NN on imbalanced Data   Figure 24: CM NB on imbalanced Data

The library of Scikit-Learn offers a confusion matrix implementation to evaluate the accuracy of a classification which can be seen above[9]. The six cells of the matrix are designated as True Negative (TN), False Negative (FN), False Positive (FP), and True Positive (TP).

As it can be seen in the classification report, RF and NN are the most appropriate DM techniques to detect fraud in unbalanced dataset. This is also confirmed by the CM of RF and NN (see figure 20 and 23). To confirm the result of classification report, false negative and false positive are considered. In RF classifier, a total of 39 and in NN a total of 37 transactions are misinterpreted. In RF, 31 fraudulent transactions are predicted as a non-fraud and 8 non-fraud transactions are predicted as a fraud. In the case of NN, 28 fraudulent transactions are predicted as a non-fraud while 9 non-fraud transactions are predicted as a fraud. The worst model on imbalanced dataset is the NB. Here 1518 fraud transactions are recognized as a non-fraud. This is also proved in the classification report, namely, the precision is very bad compared to other models.

5.8 Undersampled Data

The simplest way in an imbalanced dataset is the random undersampling of the majority class (More, 2016: 2). In the dataset, the majority class contains normal transactions, which make up 99.83 %. The minority class consists of only 0.17 % fraud transactions. There is a total of 492 fraudulent transactions in the dataset. In the next step the number of normal (non-fraud) transactions will be reduced from 284315 to 492. After this process, the data frame will contain total 984 transactions, a 50:50 proportion.

```
1.  # get fraudulent transaction indices
2.  len_fraud = len(data[data['Class']==1])
3.  indices_fraud = np.array(data[data['Class']==1].index)
4.
5.  # get normal transaction indices
6.  indices_normal = np.array(data[data['Class']==0].index)
7.  indices_normal = np.random.choice(indices_normal, len_fraud, replace=False)
8.
9.  # make a undersampled dataframe
10. undersample_indices = np.concatenate([indices_normal, indices_fraud])
11. under_df = data.iloc[undersample_indices, :]
```

For this process, the length of fraudulent transactions was assigned to class 1 *(indices_fraud)* and shortened the normal transactions to the length of the fraudulent transactions and assigned these to class 0 *(indices_normal)*. The command *random.choise* was used for that. Finally, the indices of normal transactions *(indices_normal)* and indices of fraudulent transactions *(indices_fraud)* was assigned to the data frame *under_df.*

Output:
```
Fraud transactions in undersampled Data:    492
Normal transactions in undersampled Data:   492
```

[9] Confusion Matrix in Scikit-Learn library: http://scikit-learn.org/stable/modules/generated/sklearn.metrics.confusion_matrix.html

```
Total transactions in undersampled Data:    984
Data frame shape:                           (984, 30)
```

After reducing the majority class, the data frame *under_df* contains 984 rows and 30 columns. Not to forget is the data normalization, which has already been discussed in chapter 5.2 (figure 16). Here, the data frame must also be brought into a standard scale before continuing.

The transactions are sorted in the data frame. The output of the transactions is as follows:

```
1: 205087    0    493: 251891    1
2: 24956     0    494: 251904    1
3: 58572     0    495: 252124    1
4: 240325    0    496: 252774    1
5: 112642    0    497: 254344    1
6: 158180    0    498: 254395    1
7: 104186    0    499: 255403    1
8: 9733      0    500: 255556    1
9: 12201     0    501: 258403    1
...               ...
```

Table 6: Undersampled data frame (without shuffling)

The next step is, splitting the data into train and test set. The problem will be: If 75 % of the data is used for train and 25% retain to test the model, the train set will include 50% non-fraudulent transactions and 25% fraudulent transactions. The test set for predictions, which consists of 25%, will only contain 25 % fraudulent transactions.

To solve this problem and make possible that the data is well distributed, shuffling would be a sensible approach. The *.sample* method from pandas library will be used to mix the data in the data frame and reset the index with *.reset_index* method.

```
1.  # shuffle rows in dataframe
2.  under_df = under_df.sample(frac=1).reset_index(drop=True)
```

```
0    0    974    0
1    1    975    0
2    1    976    1
3    0    977    1
4    1    978    0
5    0    979    0
6    1    980    0
7    0    981    1
8    0    982    1
9    1    983    0
...       ...
```

Table 7 Undersampled data frame (after shuffling)

The comparison between table 6 and table 7 shows, that the data in the data frame is well distributed in table 7 after shuffling so that the data can now been splitted into train and test set.

The next step is to split the data into 25/75 split in the train and test set, since this split has achieved the best results (see Chapter 5.6: Train and Test Set). The results with different split combinations on different sampling techniques were not strong. These combinations were also tried with the undersampling technique in this case study.

5.8.1 Results on undersampled Data

	Precision	Recall	F1-Score	Accuracy	Sampling type	Time in sec
Logistic Regression	0.96	0.93	0.94	0.9431	Undersampling	0
RF-Classifier	0.92	0.93	0.92	0.9309	Undersampling	0
SVM (Support Vector Classifier)	0.94	0.89	0.92	0.9146	Undersampling	0
DT (Decision Tree Classifier)	0.91	0.98	0.94	0.9390	Undersampling	0
Neural Network (MLP Classifier)	0.94	0.90	0.92	0.9228	Undersampling	0
Naïve Bayes (GaussianNB)	0.93	0.95	0.94	0.9572	Undersampling	0

Table 8: Results on undersampled data using DM techniques

At first glance in table 8 it can be seen, that all predictive models are performed better than in the first approach with imbalanced dataset. In the first approach, precision of LR, DT and NB was less than 90 %. With the undersampling technique, the precision at LR model has increased by 8 %, DT Classifier by 15 % and with NB model even by 87 %. There was also an enormous improvement in recall. Compared to the previous approach, the recall in LR is 25 % better and it also exists an improvement in DT Classifier by 23 %. Thus the probability has increased, so that there is a probability of 93 % with LR model and 98 % with DT Classifier that there is a true fraud is recognized by the classifier.

In the predictive models RF and SVM there was no major improvement in precision through in recall. In RF Classifier, the recall has increased by 19 % from 74 % to 93 %. The predictive model SVM shows also an improvement in recall by 14 %.

Precision and accuracy play a common role in a machine learning algorithm. "Precision is the proportion of the predicted positive cases that were correct", while accuracy is defined as "... the proportion of the total number of predictions that were correct" (Vafeiadis et al., 2015: 3). Therefore, both measured values must be considered together. While for the first approach, the precision for all predictive model, except NB, was greater than 99 %, it can be seen, that in this approach the accuracy in each predictive model is different. Since both measured values have a commonality, it would be incorrect to say, that machine learning with imbalanced data performed better. A predictive model is good when a high degree of precision and accuracy is achieved as well as the recall is stable.

In this approach the accuracy and precision is good in the LR and NB model compared to other models. The comparison between RF and DT Classifier shows, that although precision and accuracy are equal in both cases, the recall is better with 98 % in DT Classifier. The last choice would be the SVM algorithm. Here, the model is only 91,46 accurate while the recall is 89 % worse than other models.

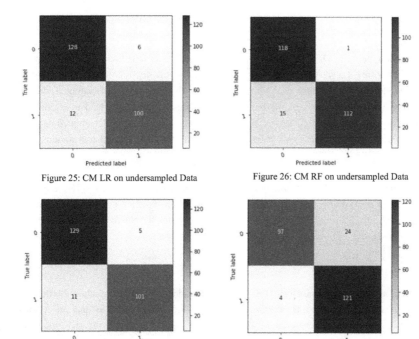

Figure 25: CM LR on undersampled Data   Figure 26: CM RF on undersampled Data

Figure 27: CM SVM on undersampled Data   Figure 28: CM DT on undersampled Data

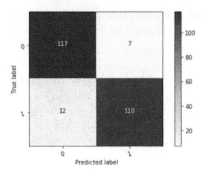

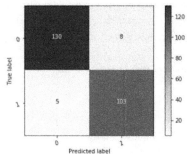

Figure 29: CM NN on undersampled Data   Figure 30: CM NB on undersampled Data

The confusion matrix of DT Classifier shows, that although only four fraud transactions were predicted as normal transactions (false negative), which is very good, but 24 normal transactions were identified as a fraud. Since in this approach the data were undersampled, the 24 transactions may still be manageable but in a large dataset, this would lead to a problem which is also cost-effective. The CM of NB model is very good in the undersampled dataset. Because only 8 normal transactions were identified as a fraud and 5 fraud transactions as a non-fraud.

The false positive and false negative counts are very similar in LR and SVM. Here only 5 transactions in SVM and 6 transactions in LR which are non-fraud are predicted as fraud. In RF Classifier, only 1 normal transaction was predicted as fraud. So, the focus in RF is on false negative counts.

5.9   Oversampled Data

In the previous approach, the majority class was downgraded to the minority class. In the case of the oversampling technique, the opposite direction will be proceeded. The data frame contains only 0.17% fraudulent transaction. These will be increased so that in the end exactly as many fraudulent transactions will be in the data frame as normal transactions.

```
1.  # get normal transaction indices
2.  len_normal = len(data[data['Class']==0])
3.  indices_normal = np.array(data[data['Class']==0].index)
4.
5.  # get fraudulent transaction indices
6.  indices_fraud = np.array(data[data['Class']==1].index)
7.  indices_fraud = np.random.choice(indices_fraud, len_normal, replace=True)
8.
9.  # make a oversampled dataframe
10. oversample_indices = np.concatenate([indices_fraud, indices_normal])
11. over_df = data.iloc[oversample_indices, :]
```

The procedure is the same as in the case of undersampling technique. Assigning normal indices to class 0 (*indices_normal*) and fraudulent indices to class 1 (*indices_fraud*). Then the fraud indices will be increased, so that in the data frame exactly as many fraudulent transactions exist as normal transactions. Again, the *random.choise* command will be used for that and the result will be saved in *over_df* data frame.

Output:

```
Fraud transaction in oversampled dataset:     284315
Normal transaction in oversampled dataset:    284315
Total oversampled data:                       568630
Data frame shape:                             (568630, 30)
```

The data frame *over_df* has now 568630 rows and 30 columns which contains 284315 normal and 284315 fraudulent transactions. Also, the data is shuffled as in undersampling approach with the *.sample* method to make a better prediction with the used machine learning techniques.

5.9.1 Results on oversampled Data

	Precision	Recall	F1-Score	Accuracy	Data	Time in sec
Logistic Regression	0.98	0.92	0.95	0.9504	Oversampling	9
RF-Classifier	1	1	1	1	Oversampling	34
SVM (Support Vector Classifier)	-	-	-	-	Oversampling	18000
DT (Decision Tree Classifier)	1	1	1	0.9998	Oversampling	18
Neural Network (MLP Classifier)	1	1	1	0.9997	Oversampling	20
Naïve Bayes (GaussianNB)	1	1	1	0.9999	Oversampling	8

Table 9: Results on oversampled data using DM techniques

It has already been mentioned in chapter 5.5 (Sampling techniques) that the oversampling technique can lead to overfitting. This approach has shown that there is overfitting in each machine learning algorithm when irrelevant independent variables are taken into the training set. This was done by randomly generating the information from the minority class (fraud transactions). It can be seen, that in LR model overfitting might not happen as strongly as with other predictive models. Another finding was that the SVM did not produce any results. After several reboots, no prediction was made with SVM. Therefore, the learning process was stopped after about five hours.

As the results in table 9 shows, that this approach is not suitable for predictions due the imbalance in the dataset, no CM was created. Since it has come to overfitting, the results were not enough meaningful in the CM.

5.10 Oversampled Data with SMOTE

As in the approach above (chapter 5.9), with random oversampled data, learning with such an imbalanced dataset is not appropriate to achieve good prediction. For that reason, in this approach the SMOTE sampling technique will be used to investigate more closely on oversampled data. In SMOTE sampling technique, the minority class will be oversampling by creating "synthetic" examples.

In the first step, the data is divided into train and test set. 75% is used for training data and 25% to test the model.

Output:
```
Length of training data:     213605
Length of test data:         71202
```

In the next step, the SMOTE technique is used to oversample the train data, which has features of *data_train_X* and labels in *data_train_y*.

```
1.  # using SMOTE function for oversampling
2.  os = SMOTE(random_state=0)
3.  # now use SMOTE to oversample our train data which
4.  # have features data_train_X and labels in data_train_y
5.  os_data_X,os_data_y=os.fit_sample(data_train_X,data_train_y)
6.  os_data_X = pd.DataFrame(data=os_data_X,columns=columns )
7.  os_data_y= pd.DataFrame(data=os_data_y,columns=["Class"])
```

With the command *fit_sample* the oversampling in the data frame can be performed. In that case *data_train_X* containing the data which have to be sampled and *data_train_y* corresponding label for each sample in *data_train_X*.

Output:
```
Length of oversampled data is:                       426438
Number of normal transaction in oversampled data:    213219
Number of fraud transaction in oversampled data:     213219
Proportion of Normal data in oversampled data is:    0.5
Proportion of fraud data in oversampled data is:     0.5
```

In the approach of random oversampling (see chapter 5.9) there are total 568630 data after oversampling. With SMOTE approach, there are now 426438 oversampled data in the data frame. The division into fraud and normal transactions is 50/50, thus there are 213219 normal and 213219 fraudulent transactions in the data frame. Not to forget is the standardization in a scale before using machine learning techniques.

5.10.1 Results on Oversampled Data with SMOTE

	Precision	Recall	F1-Score	Accuracy	Data	Time in sec
Logistic Regression	0.16	0.87	0.22	0.9896	SMOTE	6
RF-Classifier	0.90	0.79	0.84	0.9995	SMOTE	48
SVM (Support Vector Classifier)	0.63	0.73	0.68	0.9988	SMOTE	3128
DT (Decision Tree Classifier)	0.41	0.73	0.52	0.9976	SMOTE	41
Neural Network (MLP Classifier)	0.67	0.90	0.77	0.9991	SMOTE	13
Naïve Bayes (GaussianNB)	0.06	0.85	0.11	0.9767	SMOTE	2

Table 10: Results on oversampled data with SMOTE using DM techniques

In this approach, the SMOTE oversampling technique was applied, that can handle "…the class imbalance, before giving the data to the classifiers" (Seeja and Zareapoor, 2014: 7). The SMOTE technique create "synthetic" examples to oversample the minority class while in the previous approach random examples were created for oversampling. In any case, the results in table 10 show, that this sampling technique did not lead to overfitting. The reason for this is the idea of the SMOTE technique: "…form new minority examples by interpolating between samples of the same class. This has the effect of creating clusters around each minority observation" (Bernard, Heutte and Adam, 2009: 83).

Remarkable was the precision of LR (16 %) and NN (6 %) with the SMOTE technique. There is a very low probability that a true fraud in the test data is recognized by the classifier. In DT Classifier, the accuracy is very good with 99.76 % but precision and recall are not satisfying. The performance of SVM has also deteriorated compared to undersampling technique. NB and RF Classifier remained strong as in the undersampling technique and show an improvement in accuracy with 99.95 %. In both models, a high precision was achieved with the SMOTE technique. 90 % is the probability that a transaction which is classified as a fraud is truly a fraud while circa 79-80 % is the probability that a true fraud is recognized by the classifier.

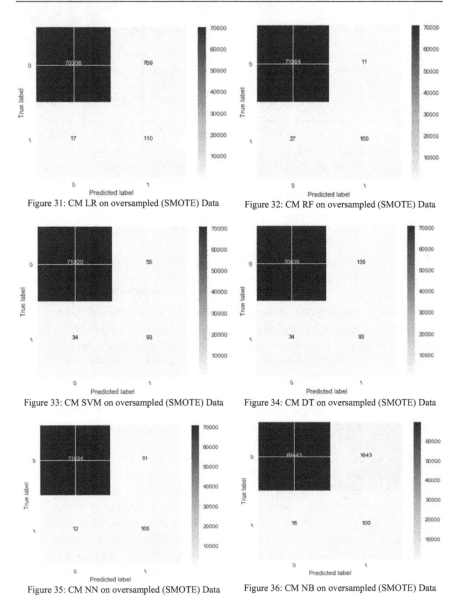

Figure 31: CM LR on oversampled (SMOTE) Data

Figure 32: CM RF on oversampled (SMOTE) Data

Figure 33: CM SVM on oversampled (SMOTE) Data

Figure 34: CM DT on oversampled (SMOTE) Data

Figure 35: CM NN on oversampled (SMOTE) Data

Figure 36: CM NB on oversampled (SMOTE) Data

As already mentioned, precision in LR and NB models is worst compared to other predictive models. This is the reason why so many false positives appear in the LR's and NB's confusion matrix. 1643 non-fraud transactions with NB and 769 non-fraud transactions with LR model are predicted as a fraud. DT Classifier is not much better and predicted 136 normal transactions as a fraud. The other techniques are not bad but not competent as the RF Classifi-er, which achieved best results. The CM of RF (figure 32) shows, that only 11 non-fraud transactions were predicted as a fraud and 27 fraud transactions as a non-fraud.

The approach with undersampled data contained only 246 transactions in the test set. In this approach the dataset is 280 times larger with 71202 transactions in the test set. From this fact it can be concluded that the SMOTE oversampling technique is suitable to deal with a large dataset. The result of classification report (see table 10) has shown that RF Classifier is very suitable for making predictions in such a dataset.

5.11 Undersampled Data with Hyperparameters Optimization

Until now, six machine learning models (LR, RF, SVM, DT, NN and NB) were used in four different data types (imbalanced, oversampled, undersampled and oversampled with SMOTE). Firstly the learning and detecting of fraud on imbalanced data will be considered from the point of view and focused on the remaining three sampling techniques. In the case of the random oversampling technique, the conclusion was, that learning with used DM tech-niques leads to overfitting. The reason for this was the small number of fraud transactions in the imbalanced dataset, which was simply multiplied. With SMOTE, another oversampling technique, better prediction was achieved. In general, it can be said that the best result was achieved through the undersampling technique. The prediction was better in comparison to other sampling techniques.

In considering how to make machine learning with the various DM techniques more efficient, it was found that optimization of hyperparameters is a good way to increase the performance. In the previous approaches, all models with standard parameters were used, it means, no op-timization of the hyperparameters has been carried out so far. In machine learning, different values exist for hyperparameters and are trained differently on the models. With the best cho-sen hyperparameters it is possible to increase the performance.

5.11.1 Model Parameter and Hyperparameter

Before continuing, it is important to understand the difference between model parameter and hyperparameter. "A model parameter is a configuration variable that is internal to the model and whose value can be estimated from data", while "(a) model hyperparameter is a configu-ration that is external to the model and whose value cannot be estimated from data." (Brown-lee, 2017). The model parameters are not set manually by the practitioner; they are estimated or learned from the data required in the predictions (ibid.). The model hyperparameters are given by the practitioner and are often used in processes to estimate the model parameters (ibid.). The hyperparameters help to recognize the modelling problem and to achieve better result by optimization.

In machine learning, "… a common tradeoff is between model accuracy and speed of making a prediction." (Tartakovsky, Clark and McCourt, 2017). The optimization of hyperparameters has advantages as well as disadvantages. One advantage for example would be that by optimizing the model perform better. A disadvantage would be that learning on the model is slowed down and thus requires more time, which can be cost-effective.

As already mentioned, the prediction with undersampled data achieved so far best results, so the hyperparameter optimization also will be done on undersampled data. In the undersampled data frame there are 492 fraudulent and 492 normal transactions, not so much data, so learning should not be slowed down. The goal of this approach is to achieve better prediction in undersampled data with hyperparameter optimization.

5.11.2 Hyperparameter optimization algorithms

In many literatures, the authors mention various hyperparameters optimization algorithms. The most frequently mentioned are Random Search and Grid Search (Huang *et al.*, 2007: 335; Hsu, Chang and Lin, 2016: 5; Witten *et al.*, 2016: 324). Both optimization algorithms, GridSearchCV and RandomizedSearchCV, are also available in Scikit-Learn, a Machine Learning library for Python programming language[10]. GridSearchCV considers given values for all parameter combinations. RadomizedSearchCV, on the other hand, considers a given number of candidates from a parameter space with a specified distribution (ibid.). Both types of algorithms found in Scikit-Learn end with CV. It is the abbreviation for cross-validation (Hsu, Chang and Lin, 2016: 5).

5.11.3 Explanation of selected Hyperparameters

In the following table the hyperparameters are listed for each DM technique used for the optimization. All parameters executed in the table were used by the Machine Learning Library of Scikit-Learn

Model	Parameter	Selected values
LogisticRegression	penalty	"l1", "l2"
	C	0.001, 0.01, 0.1, 1, 10
	solver	'liblinear'
	cv	10
RandomForestClassifier and DecisionTreeClassifier	max_depth	3, None
	max_features	1, 3, 10
	min_samples_split	2, 4, 10
	min_samples_leaf	1, 3, 10
	criterion	"gini", "entropy"
	n_estimators	100

---

[10] Tuning the hyper-parameters of an estimator. See: http://scikit-learn.org/stable/modules/grid_search.html

	cv	10
	kernel	"rbf"
SVM	C	0.1, 1, 10, 100, 1000
(Support Vector Classifier)	gamma	0.1, 0.01, 0.001, 0.0001, 0.00001
	cv	10
	solver	"lbfgs", "sgd", "adam"
NN	alpha	0.0001, 0.001, 0.01, 0.1
(MLP-Classifier)	hidden_layer_sizes	2, 10, 50, 100
	cv	10

Table 11: Selected values of hyperparameters for optimization

In LR, three hyperparameters were selected for optimization. L1 and L2 are two different regularization methods, that can be applied to prevent overfitting and to achieve better predictions (Ng, 2004: 1). L1 regularization basically minimizes the sum of the absolute differences between the target value and the predicted value (ibid.). L2 regularization works similar and minimizes the sum of the square of the differences between the target value and predicted values (ibid.). *L1* and *L2* penalty have different effects on parameter *C* in LR. This allows the comparison of the sparsity to be made. Sparsity refers to the fact that very few matrix or vector are not equal to zero (Lo, 2013). In a comparison of Scikt-Learn[11], it can be seen, that large values of *C* parameters give more freedom to the model, while smaller values constrain the model more (ibid.). Another hyperparameter used in LR classifier, is the solver.

Following solvers are available in the Scikit-learn library: *newton-cg, saga, sag, liblinear, lbfgs*.

Solvers like *newton-cg, sag* and *lbfgs* can only handle *L2* penalty. Since in this approach both L-regularization methods are used only *saga* and *liblinear* solver come into consideration. *Liblinear* solver is a good choice for small data set and can handle both L-regularization methods, where saga solver is suitable for large datasets. Another point is the optimization of the hyperparameter which is tested in this approach on undersampled data. From this view, it is sufficient to use the solver *liblinear*.

In SVM classifier, two known kernels are often used to solve the classification problem. The radial basis function (*RBF*) kernel and *linear* kernel, where the *RBF* kernel is mostly the first choice (Huang and Wang, 2006: 231; Hsu, Chang and Lin, 2016: 2,3,4). In this study, RBF-kernel-function is used for hyperparameter optimization with grid search. This kernel maps the samples nonlinearly to a higher dimensional space and can analyse the data in the case where the relationship between class labels and attributes is nonlinear.

Furthermore, two parameters must be defined (*C* and *gamma*) when using the mentioned RBF-kernel (Wu, Tzeng and Lin, 2009: 4726). The aim is to find the best values for *C* and *gamma* in the RBF-kernel (Ahmad *et al.*, 2004: 313). The cost parameter *C* controls the pen-

---

[11] cf. (L1 Penalty and Sparsity in Logistic Regression) in http://scikit-learn.org/stable/auto_examples/linear_model/plot_logistic_l1_l2_sparsity.html

alty paid for misclassification of training examples against simplicity of the decision surface. The *gamma* parameter defines how far the influence of a single training examples reaches (Huang, Lu and Ling, 2003: 2,3 & Karatzoglou, Meyer and Hornik, 2005: 3). The goal of a high cost value C is to create a complex enough prediction function and classify all training examples correctly while a low cost value C leads to a simpler prediction function (Karatzoglou, Meyer and Hornik, 2005: 3).

As already mentioned, RF and DT classifiers works very similar. Both techniques were used to compare with each other. For this, the selection of the hyperparameters must also be the same. The hyperparameter criterion in RF and DT classifiers are used as a function to measure the quality of a split. Supported criteria mention in Scikit-Learn library are *gini* for the *gini impurity* and *entropy* for the information gain, which are tree-specific. If all samples in the dataset belong to the same class at a node, the *entropy* will be equal to zero and for a uniform class distribution the *entropy* will be maximal (Raschka, n.d.). The *gini* impurity is very similar to *entropy* criteria and is maximum when the classes are perfectly mixed (ibid.). The *gini* impurity can be viewed as a criterion that attempts to reduce misclassification (ibid.).
The *n_estimator* defines the number of trees in the RF classifier and has the default value 10. In this approach the value of the number of trees is set to 100. Other hyperparameters used in RF and DT (*max_depth, max_features, min_samples_split, min_samples_leaf*) control the size of the trees. This can cause the trees to become very complex and large for some datasets, so that a lot of memory is consumed and the performance is not well enough. The parameter values selected in table 11 can be choose differently for each split. The best value for the respective parameter is used for each split to hold on an improvement.

In MLP Classifier, three solver hyperparameters will be used: *SGD, L-BFGS* and *ADAM*. According to Le et. al (2011: 265-266) SGD solver (Stochastic Gradient Descent) is widely used in deep learning and is easy to implement but it is computationally expensive because of their many times optimization procedure. L-BFGS (Limited memory BGFS) solver is more stable to train and more powerful than SGD but more suitable for small datasets (ibid.). ADAM is used in Scikit-Learn library as default solver in MLP Classifier and works perfectly on large datasets.
The hidden layers represent the number of neurons (Yoo *et al.*, 2012: 2434-2435). With the selection of the hidden layers, the classification performance can be influenced very quickly (ibid.). The hyperparameter *alpha* used the L2 regularization method and "… can be proposed for preventing overfitting in neuronal networks" (Srivastava *et al.*, 2014: 1942).

In table 11, Gaussian Naïve Bayes algorithm was not executed, because this technique does not have any hyperparameters that can be tuned (Alvari, Shakarian and Snyder, 2017: 9; Olson *et al.*, 2017: 4).

5.11.4 Cross-Validation

It is common to use the holdout method for a limited amount of data. In the holdout method, the data is divided so that a certain amount is used for the test and the remainder is used for the training (Witten *et al.*, 2016: 152). For example, in the previous approaches, 75% were used for training and 25% for testing. It is possible, that the sample which was used for the training is not representative (ibid.). To ensure representativeness, each class from the dataset must be in the right proportion in the training- and test set. In the case of credit card fraud, the class is filled with 0 and 1. While class with the value 0 is a normal transaction, class 1 is known for a fraud. And exactly this partition, must be represented in the training and test set in an approximately equal proportion (ibid.: 153). For this, the technique called cross-validation can be used (ibid.). During the cross-validation, you can define a fixed number of folds or in other words partitions yourself (ibid.). In many literatures, a 10-fold cross valida-tion is often used or recommended (Kirkos, Spathis and Manolopoulos, 2007: 1002; Weiss, Indurkhya and Zhang, 2010: 72 & Witten *et al.*, 2016: 153). In a 10-fold cross validation the data is split into 10 approximately equal partitions (Witten *et al.*, 2016: 153). In that case 90 % of data is used for training and 10 % for testing. This procedure is repeated 10 times "… so that in the end, every instance has been used exactly once for testing" (ibid.). If we transfer the strategy to the dataset of credit card fraud, it can be assumed, that each fold contains an equal number of fraud and non-fraud cases.

Apart from the performance enhancement, a further advantage is that "(t)he cross-validation procedure can prevent the overfitting problem." (Hsu, Chang and Lin, 2016: 5). A downside of cross-validation is, that the procedure takes more time. For example, in a 10-fold cross-validation, the procedure is repeated 10 times, which requires more time in comparison to one training set.

5.11.5 Selection of Hyperparameter Optimization Algorithm and k-fold CV

In this approach GridSearchCV algorithm from Scikit-Learn and 10-fold cross-validation is used. While search for literatures and tutorials with CV, many authors and practitioners con-sider a 5-fold and 10-fold CV as useful (Kirkos, Spathis and Manolopoulos, 2007: 1002; Weiss, Indurkhya and Zhang, 2010: 72; Witten *et al.*, 2016: 153 & Raschka, 2016). The con-clusion was, however, that in several researches a 10-fold CV delivers better results and is more robust (ibid.).

In this case study, the tests on Logistic Regression and Random Forest Classifiers, 10-fold CV achieves better results than with 5-fold CV. These tests were run with RandomizedSearchCV and GridSearchCV. On both hyperparameter optimization algorithms the division into 10-fold CV was better.

In many literatures it is mentioned that Random Search is more effective than Grid Search (Bergstra and Yoshua, 2012: 281 & Deep, 2015), but there is no clear evidence. Therefore, both optimization algorithms were used on LR and RF model. After learning, the two algorithms were compared and the better one selected for further process.

The following steps were executed:

1. The undersampled data was divided into training and test data as well as in other approaches.
2. Various hyperparameters were tested on both optimization algorithms using LR and RF as learning techniques and the CV parameter was set to 10 for 10-fold CV.
3. After the execution, the hyperparameters were selected which have performed best and subsequently the learning was used on the complete training set with the best hyperparameters optimization and predicted on test data set.
4. The steps above, were repeated five times and then the mean of precision, recall and accuracy were calculated.

| Procedure | Logistic Regression | | | | | |
| | GridSearchCV | | | RandomizedSearchCV | | |
	Precision	Recall	AUC	Precision	Recall	AUC
1.	0.95	0.94	0.9431	0.97	0.91	0.9431
2.	0.99	0.95	0.9715	0.94	0.92	0.9390
3.	0.97	0.89	0.9268	0.95	0.92	0.9350
4.	0.96	0.95	0.9512	0.97	0.93	0.9553
5.	0.96	0.93	0.9472	0.97	0.93	0.9512
Mean	0.97	0.93	0.9480	0.96	0.93	0.9447

Table 12: Model selection for hyperparameter optimization on LR

| Procedure | Random Forest | | | | | |
| | GridSearchCV | | | RandomizedSearchCV | | |
	Precision	Recall	AUC	Precision	Recall	AUC
1.	0.99	0.91	0.9472	0.98	0.91	0.9472
2.	0.97	0.90	0.9309	1.00	0.84	0.9228
3.	1.00	0.93	0.9634	0.96	0.94	0.9472
4.	0.99	0.89	0.9350	0.99	0.87	0.9268
5.	0.98	0.96	0.9593	0.92	0.96	0.9431
Mean	0.99	0.92	0.9471	0.97	0.93	0.9374

Table 13: Model selection for hyperparameter optimization on RF

Table 12 and table 11 above show that there is not much difference between GridSearchCV and RandomizedSearchCV in Logistic Regression. In both models, there is an average Recall of 93%. In Precision and Accuracy, there is a minimal improvement by using Grid Search algorithm can be seen.

In Random Forest, the sensitivity (Recall) has fallen by 1%, but Precision and Accuracy are better when using Grid Search algorithm. Another finding was, that the use of Grid Search algorithm slows down learning in comparison with random undersampling technique. The time would play an important role in larger datasets. For the further process the Grid Search algorithm is used for optimizing the hyperparameters because a better performance was shown by the test above.

5.11.6 Results on Undersampled Data with Hyperparameter Optimization

	Precision	Recall	F1-Score	Accuracy	Sampling + Optimization Algorithm	Time in sec
Logistic Regression	0.97	0.93	0.95	0.9480	Undersampling, GridSearchCV	0
RF-Classifier	0.99	0.92	0.95	0.9471	Undersampling, GridSearchCV	55
SVM (Support Vector Classifier)	0.97	0.92	0.95	0.9472	Undersampling, GridSearchCV	207
DT (Decision Tree Classifier)	0.96	0.86	0.91	0.9081	Undersampling, GridSearchCV	10
Neural Network (MLP Classifier)	0.96	0.90	0.93	0.9431	Undersampling, GridSearchCV	45

Table 14: Results on undersampled data after parameter tuning

Table 14 shows the results of classification report with hyperparameters optimization in an undersampled dataset. The goal of this approach was to improve the precision, recall and accuracy by optimizing the hyperparameters in the respective machine learning models. Compared to undersampling approach, where the standard parameters were used, there is an improvement after hyperparameter optimization process. Although the selection of hyperparameters is not easy and requires a lot of time, the result is clearly visible. In LR model, the precision has improved by 1 % and accuracy has increased also by about half percent. In RF classifier, there was a clear improvement in precision. The recall in RF classifier has fallen by 1 percent, but the precision has increased by a good 7 % to 99 % while the accuracy also increased by half percent.

The result of SVM also shows an improvement in accuracy (before: 91.46%, afterwards: 94.72%) but also in precision and recall. Something notable was the measure of accuracy recall in DT classifier. Here the recall fell by 12 % and there was also a retreat in accuracy (before 93.90%, afterwards: 90.81%). It should also be noted, that the hyperparameters used in RF- and DT Classifier were same and were selected to compare each other. It could be possible to achieve an improvement through the correct selection of hyperparameters in DT classifier.

The result of MLP classifier also revealed an improvement of 2 % in precision and about two percent in accuracy. Since only three hyperparameters were used in this approach and the classifier offers more hyperparameters for tuning, it cannot be ruled out that the result can be even better by selecting several hyperparameters.

5.12 Review of the case study: Credit Card Fraud Detection

Looking back at chapter 5, several machine learning algorithms were used to discover fraud in credit card dataset, provided by Kaggle[12]. For this, six different Data Mining techniques – Logistic Regression, Random Forest, Support Vector Machine, Decision Tree, Neural Networks and Naïve Bayes – were used. The description and selection of the individual DM techniques can be found in chapter 5.4.

The used dataset contains a very high percentage (99.83 %) of normal transactions and a very low percentage (0.17 %) of fraud transactions, thus the dataset for the investigation was very imbalanced. To deal with such a dataset, some sampling techniques were mentioned in chapter 5.5 (Sampling techniques), which were later used. The use of DM techniques to build model can predict future outcomes started mainly in chapter 5.6 (Train and Test Set). In this chapter, the goal was to determine the correct split for the train and test set used for the classification model. The result showed (chapter 5.6) that in this case the 75/25 split was most suitable with different sampling techniques.

The result of the individual DM techniques was presented in a classification report and confusion matrix, which are available in Scikit-Learn library. Both are used for describing the performance in a classification model (chapter 5.3 Confusion Matrix Terminology).

The result has shown that the best precision, recall and accuracy were achieved by using an undersampling technique in an imbalanced dataset. In the random oversampling technique, all predictive models have led to overfitting. A better way for oversampling was the SMOTE oversampling technique, but the result in the classification report showed, that the performance has decreased very much. To improve the predictions further and achieve better precision, recall and accuracy, an optimization of the hyperparameters were carried out in the predictive models. Two hyperparameters optimization algorithms – Grid Search and Randomized

---

[12] Credit card fraud dataset available at: https://www.kaggle.com/dalpozz/creditcardfraud

Search – were available for this purpose. Both algorithms were tested on Logistic Regression and Random Forest Classifiers. The result has shown, that while both are relatively well suited, Grid Search algorithm shows a little better performance. The selection of the used hyperparameters was explained in chapter 5.11.3. In addition to the optimization of the hyperparameters the 10-fold cross validation was used to split the train and test sets in equal proportion. The complex optimization in the last approach has shown that the selection of the hyperparameters makes learning better.

6 Conclusion

White-collar crime or said in other words economic crime is a highly topical issue today. Many companies are affected by white-collar crime every year and it is difficult for them to identify the damage caused by fraudulent activity. In this thesis, the well-known types of white-collar crime related to financial fraud have been treated in more detail. Furthermore, it was demonstrated by the fraud triangle of Cressey (chapter 2.2), which factors must come together in the development of white-collar crime.

Big Data is characterized by the fact, that data is mostly semi-structured or unstructured. With digitalization and economic change, the data is growing daily and it is becoming difficult for companies to monitor it. To detect white-collar crime, it is also important to analyse unstructured data, which make up to 80 % in a company. To analyse the unstructured data, it must first be transformed and pre-processed in a structured way. For this purpose, the example in the thesis used two self-generated e-mails to illustrate how textual data can be converted into numeric values and weighted with Term-Frequency – Inverse Document Frequency (TD-IDF) to apply that data to predictive Data Mining techniques. Furthermore, the emerging trend in the industry through the application of DM techniques was treated in this thesis. For this a case study for detecting fraud in a highly imbalanced and anonymous credit card transactions dataset was carried out. A literature search was performed to select the DM techniques and different sampling techniques were applied to solve the class imbalance problem.

The results with the undersampling technique are summarized in table 6 and figure 25 to 30. Based on the accuracy measure it can concluded that the best model in this approach is Naïve Bayes (GaussianNB) with the highest predictive accuracy of 95.72 % followed by Logistic Regression (LR) with predictive accuracy of 94.31 %. Random Forest (RF) and Decision Tree (DT) have a similar prediction accuracy (93.09 % or. 93.90 %), but a deeper look into the results of confusion matrix (figure 26 and 28) shows that DT predicts 24 non-fraud transactions as a fraud while RF Classifier predicts only one non-fraud transaction as a fraud. Considering false positive observations, it can be said, that in RF Classifier 15 fraud transactions were predicted by the Classifier as non-frauds and only 4 fraud transactions with the DT Classifier were predicted as a non-fraud. A total of 16 transactions with RF and 28 transactions with DT were misclassified. With this observation, it can be said, that RF performs better than DT Classifier despite a slightly lower prediction accuracy.
MLP Classifier (NN) has the second lowest prediction accuracy of 92.28% and Support Vector Classifier (SVM) has the lowest accuracy of 91.46 %. Also, the evaluation measure recall is very bad here with 89 % (SVM) and 90 % (NN) compared to other models.

With the oversampling approach in this thesis, no results could be achieved (table 9). It was found that all six used DM techniques led to overfitting. A better approach is the SMOTE oversampling. In this approach the minority class was oversampled by creating synthetic examples. The results with SMOTE approach (table 10) were not as good as with undersampling approach, but much better than random oversampling because this approach did not lead to overfitting. While the predictive accuracy was better than in undersampling approach, it was found that other evaluation measures – precision, recall and F1-score scored lower in all models. RF Classifier achieved the highest predictive accuracy of 99.95 % and the highest precision of 90 % followed by MLP Classifier (NN) with predictive accuracy of 99.91 % and precision of 67 %. The third best model was the SVM in this approach with predictive accuracy of 63 %. In all other models, the precision was lower than 50 % (LR: 16 %, DT: 41 %, NB: 6 %). Based on the F-measure in this approach RF and NN are appropriate DM techniques which have also a low false positive and false negative rate (figure 32 and 35).

In the last approach, the Grid Search algorithm was used on the undersampled data to improve the predictive model with the hyperparameter optimization. The NB Classifier was not considered in this approach because this model does not provide any hyperparameters for tuning. Moreover, 10-k cross validation was used to divide the data in right proportion. The goal was to increase the predictive accuracy and other evaluation measures. The results show (table 14), that an improvement in RF Classifier and SVM has been achieved. The predictive accuracy increased by 1.62 % in RF and 3.26 % in Support Vector Classifier. Remarkably, the precision has increased in all 5 models. On the other hand, the recall values have fallen in RF, DT and NN. As well, the predictive accuracy in LR, DT and NN has decreased. It should be mentioned, that the selection of hyperparameter for the optimization was selected based on existing literatures and best practices. Therefore, it is not excluded that a further improvement can be achieved in the used DM techniques.

Based on the experience with Text Mining (TM) approach and case study on credit card fraud detection, the research question is answered as follows:
The seven practice areas of Text Mining are necessary for understanding to solve the problem of unstructured data. Information Retrieval is used to search and retrieve large text databases. Information Extraction deals with constructing structured data from unstructured text with the aim to extract meaningful information. After the unstructured text is transformed in a structured form the next practice area of TM can applied which is Document Clustering. This is an algorithm of DM and an unsupervised learning method which is used to group similar documents into a cluster. Document Classification has the goal to classify known examples from train set and categorize unknown examples automatically. Natural Language Processing capture the meaning of the investigated text while Web Mining, the last practice area of TM, deals with the extraction of meaningful information from WWW.

Based on the exercise in TM chapter (4.3.2) it was clear, that data pre-processing is the first step in TM approach. With the steps of transformation, cleaning, tokenization, filtering and stemming the data can be transferred in a structured from. Term matrix can help to transform words into numerical values and with the approach "Term-Frequency" the terms can be weighted by importance. Afters these steps, the data is in a structured from and can be applied on predictive DM techniques.

Based on the case study in this thesis, it can be concluded that NB, LR and RF are the most appropriate DM techniques to solve classification problems. In all sampling techniques approaches, RF Classifier achieved a good predictive accuracy, precision and recall. NB and LR are not suitable in large datasets according to SMOTE Oversampling approach. Here the precision in both models was very low. RF, NN and SVM shows that these techniques are well suitable to solve classification problems in large datasets. One disadvantage of SVM was, that this algorithm took long processing time in all approaches and the result was not better than RF Classifier which was much faster in processing. The result of DT Classifier was in all approaches worse compared to other DM techniques, therefore it should not be given so much attention in further research.

The aim of the present work was to gain first insights into a classification problem in the credit card dataset and present appropriate DM techniques. It has become clear, that the obtained results differ in some cases from previously existing literatures, studies and best practises. The reasons for this may be that different datasets are applied to the machine learning algorithms and that these techniques work differently on datasets. Therefore, it would be wrong to say that the DM techniques examined in this thesis will show the same accuracy on all other datasets.

In this work, only one dataset was used and different sampling techniques were applied to interpret the analysis results of used DM techniques. Other aspects such as important loss of important information in undersampling approach were not considered. It is important for the user or data analyst to define the goal from the business understanding phase properly. He must also invest a lot of time in the data understanding and data preparation phase. The three phases of the CRISP-DM reference model are basic requirements to achieve qualitative results at the end of the DM project.

In addition to that, it could be found that Text Mining approach for unstructured data is very complex and can take a lot of time. In this thesis, only two self-generated e-mails were selected as examples and did show that data pre-processing, term matrix and term-frequency are required to transfer unstructured data in a structured form. However, other approaches or techniques that may not be as complex as the present approach were untended. For the further research, it could be investigated, which other procedures exists to transfer unstructured text in structured from.

In many studies and literatures there is a connection between TM and DM by interpreting the research results but there is still a lack of best practices in this area which show how to apply data to predictive DM techniques after using TM approach.

For further research - fraud detection in unstructured data - the ENRON email dataset is recommended. The insolvency of ENRON in December 2001 left debts of about 40 billion dollars and is one of the biggest bankruptcy in the US company history (Böhm, 2003). The data was released by the Federal Energy Regulatory Commission and it is the only scientific dataset. In the dataset, email data from more than 150 employees with 500.000 email messages of Enron are included. The dataset is available at: https://www.cs.cmu.edu/~enron/.

7 Sources

Aggarwal, C. C., & Zhai, C. (2012). A Survey of Text Clustering Algorithms. In: Aggarwal C., Zhai C. (eds) Mining Text Data. Springer, Boston, MA.

Ahmad, A. R., Khalia, M., Viard-Gaudin, C., & Poisson, E. (2004). Online handwriting recognition using support vector machine. In TENCON 2004. 2004 IEEE Region 10 Conference (Vol. A, p. 311–314 Vol. 1).

Akosa, J. S. (2017). Predictive Accuracy: A Misleading Performance Measure for Highly Imbalanced Data.

Albashrawi, M., & Lowell, M. (2016). Detecting Financial Fraud Using Data Mining Techniques, Journal of Data Science, 14(3), 553–570.

Albon, C., (2016) Machine Learning – Precision, Recall and F1-Scores, Internet notes, published on 2016 Mai, viewed on 13th September 2017, from https://chrisalbon.com/machine-learning/precision_recall_and_F1_scores.html

Alvari, H., Shakarian, P., & Snyder, J. E. K. (2017). Semi-supervised learning for detecting human trafficking. Security Informatics, 6(1), 1.

AuditFactory (2013). Anti Fraud Management System. Retrieved from http://www.forum-executives.de/beitrag-detail/article/anti-fraud-management-system-ein-ueberblick.html (viewed 30th July 2017).

Basari, A. S. H., Hussin, B., Ananta, I. G. P., & Zeniarja, J. (2013). Opinion mining of movie review using hybrid method of support vector machine and particle swarm optimization. In Procedia Engineering (Vol. 53, pp. 453–462).

Bergstra, J., & Yoshua, B. (2012). Random Search for Hyper-Parameter Optimization. Journal of Machine Learning Research, 13, 281–305.

Bernard, S., Heutte, L., & Adam, S. (2009). Influence of hyperparameters on random forest accuracy. In Lecture Notes in Computer Science (including subseries Lecture Notes in Artificial Intelligence and Lecture Notes in Bioinformatics), 5519 LNCS, 171–180.

Bhattacharyya, S., Jha, S., Tharakunnel, K., & Westland, J. C. (2011). Data mining for credit card fraud: A comparative study. Decision Support Systems, 50(3), 602–613.

Biegelman, M. T., & Bartow, J. T. (2012). Executive Roadmap to Fraud Prevention and Internal Control. Chapter 2: Fraud Theory and Prevention (2nd ed.). John Wiley & Sons, Incorporated.

Blakehead. (2013). Fraud detection – the unstructured data goldmine. Retrieved from http://www.blakehead.co.uk/user_uploads/fraud_detection_-_the_unstructured_data_goldmine.pdf (viewed on 20th September 2017)

Bohlander, M., (2016). German Criminal Code. Retrieved from https://www.gesetze-im-internet.de/englisch_stgb/englisch_stgb.html_-_p2173 (viewed 20th July 2017).

Böhm, A. (2003). Der Enron Skandal – Ein Lehrstück über Wirtschaftskriminalität, Online article. Retrieved from https://www.cilip.de/2003/02/07/der-enron-skandal-ein-lehrstueck-ueber-wirtschaftskriminalitaet/_-_ftnref1 (viewed on 27th November 2017).

Bollacker, Kurt D.; Lawrence, Steve; Giles, C. Lee (1998). "CiteSeer: An Autonomous Web Agent for Automatic Retrieval and Identification of Interesting Publications". Proceedings of the Second International Conference on Autonomous Agents. AGENTS '98. New York, NY, USA: ACM: 116–123.

Böttner, (n.d.). Strafverteidigung im Wirtschaftsstrafrecht. Retrieved from http://www.wirtschaftsstrafrecht-strafverteidiger.de/vermoegensdelikte/ (viewed on 20th July 2017).

Bouchachia, A. (2014). Adaptive and Intelligent Systems, Third International Conference, ICAIS 2014, Bournemouth, UK, September 8-10, 2014. Proceedings (3rd ed.). UK: Springer International Publishing.

Buonaguidi , B. (2017). Credit card fraud: What you need to know. Oline article. Retrieved from http://www.bbc.com/capital/story/20170711-credit-card-fraud-what-you-need-to-know (viewed on 29th July 2017)

Boys, C. (2017). Detecting credit card fraud in Python, Internet Blog, published on 2017 February. Retrieved from http://www.clintonboys.com/kaggle-cc-fraud/ (viewed on 11th September 2017).

Brause, R., Langsdorf, T., & Hepp, M. (2010). Neural data mining for credit card fraud detection. J.W.Goethe-University, Frankfurt A. M.

Brownlee, J., (2017). What is the Difference Between a Parameter and a Hyperparameter?, Internet article, Machine Learning Mastery, published on 2017 July. Retrieved from https://machinelearningmastery.com/difference-between-a-parameter-and-a-hyperparameter/ (viewed on 23th September 2017).

Bundeskriminalamt (2015). Wirtschaftskriminalität Bundeslagebild 2015. Wiesbaden.

Bundeskriminalamt (2016). Wirtschaftskriminalität Bundeslagebild 2016. Wiesbaden.

Buonaguidi, B. (2017). Credit Card Fraud: What you need to know, published by BBC on 2017 July. Retrieved from http://www.bbc.com/capital/story/20170711-credit-card-fraud-what-you-need-to-know (viewed on 13th August 2017).

Cano J. (2014). The V's of Big Data: Velocity, Volume, Value, Variety, and Veracity. Published on 2014 March. Retrieved from https://www.xsnet.com/blog/bid/205405/The-V-s-of-Big-Data-Velocity-Volume-Value-Variety-and-Veracity (viewed on 17th August 2017).

Chartered Global Management Accountant (ed.) (2012). Fraud Risk Management: A guide to good practise. Retrieved from http://www.cgma.org/Resources/Reports/Downloadable-Documents/fraudriskmanagement.pdf (viewed on 5th August 2017).

Chartered Institute of Management Accountants (ed.) (2009). Fraud Risk Management - A guide to good practice. Retrieved from http://www.cimaglobal.com/Documents/ImportedDocuments/cid_techguide_fraud_risk_management_feb09.pdf.pdf (viewed on 5th August 2017).

Chaudhuri, S., Dayal, U., & Narasayya, V. (2011). An overview of business intelligence technology. Communications of the ACM, 54 (8).

Chen, R.-C., Shu-Ting, L., & Shiue-Shiun, L. (2006). Detecting Credit Card Fraud by Using Support Vector Machines and Neural Networks. International Journal of Soft Computing, 1(1), 30–35.

Creditreform (2016a). Insolvenzen in Deutschland, Jahr 2016. Nuess. Retrieved from https://www.creditreform.de/nc/aktuelles/news-list/details/news-detail/insolvenzen-in-deutschland-jahr-2016-3303.html

Creditreform (2016b). Wirtschaftslage und Finanzierung im Mittelstand, Herbst 2016. Creditreform Presse- Und Öffentlichkeitsarbeit, 1–4.

Dal Pozzolo, A. (2015). Adaptive Machine Learning for Credit Card Fraud Detection. Computer Science Department Machine Learning Group.

Dang, D. S., Ahmad, P. H. (2015). A review of text mining techniques associated with various application areas, International Journal of Science and Research (IJSR), 4(2).

Deep, A. E., (2015). Smarter Parameter Sweeps (or Why Grid Search Is Plain Stupid), Internet Article, Medium, published on 2015 June. Retrieved from https://medium.com/rants-on-machine-learning/smarter-parameter-sweeps-or-why-grid-search-is-plain-stupid-c17d97a0e881 (viewed on 25th September 2017).

Dhanapal, R., & Gayathiri P. (2012). Credit Card Fraud Detection using Decision Tree for tracing Email and IP. IJCSI International Journal of Computer Science, 9(5).

Diversy, J., & Weyand, R. (2013). Insolvenzdelikte: Unternehmenszusammenbruch und Strafrecht (9th ed.). Berlin : Erich Schmidt.

Dubey, R., Zhou, J., Wang, Y., Thompson, P. M., & Ye, J. (2014). Analysis of sampling techniques for imbalanced data: An n=648 ADNI study. NeuroImage, 87, 220–241.

EHFCN. (2010). EHFCN Annual Report 2009/2010. Retrieved from http://www2.mz.gov.pl/wwwfiles/ma_struktura/docs/ar_may2010_final_email.pdf

(viewed on 16th August 2017).

Fawcett, T., (2016). Learning from Imbalanced Classes, Internet News, KDnuggets News, published on 2016 August. Retrieved from http://www.kdnuggets.com/2016/08/learning-from-imbalanced-classes.html/2 (viewed on 19th September 2017).

FAZ (2016). Betrüger erbeuten mit Chef-Masche über 100 Millionen Euro. Retrieved from http://www.faz.net/aktuell/wirtschaft/unternehmen/wirtschaftskriminalitaet-betrueger-erbeuten-mit-chef-masche-ueber-100-millionen-euro-14398951.html (viewed on 31th October 2017).

FICO (2015). FICO Data Shows Credit Card Fraud Rising in Germany, published on 2015 May in Munich. Retrieved from http://www.fico.com/en/newsroom/fico-data-shows-credit-card-fraud-rising-in-germany-05-07-2015 (viewed on 13th August 2017).

Gaikwad, S. V., Y Patil, P. D., & Patil, P. (2014). Text Mining Methods and Techniques. International Journal of Computer Applications, 85(17), 975–8887.

Gartner (2017) Data Mining, Online Article. Retrieved from https://www.gartner.com/it-glossary/data-mining (viewed on 22th October 2017).

Gharehchopogh, F. S., & Khalifelu, Z. A. (2011). Analysis and evaluation of unstructured data: Text mining versus natural language processing. 2011 5th International Conference on Application of Information and Communication Technologies (AICT), (May 2014), 1–4.

Gleim, I. N. (2008). Study Unit Ten Engagement Procedures, Ethics, and Fraud. Gleim Publications. Retrieved from http://auditbooks.weebly.com/uploads/4/0/6/9/4069797/10._-engagement_procedures_ethics_fraud.pdf (viwed on 10th August 2017)

Gupta, R., & Gill, N. S. (2012). Financial Statement Fraud Detection using Text Mining. International Journal of Advanced Computer Science and Applications, 3(12), 189–191.

Halim, A., Omar, B., Omar, A. H., Najib, M., & Salleh, M. (2013). Modeling Unstructured Document Using N-gram Consecutive and WordNet Dictionary. IJCSI International Journal of Computer Science Issues, Vol. 10(2).

Hashimi, H., Hafez, A., & Mathkour, H. (2015). Selection criteria for text mining approaches. Computers in Human Behavior, 51, 729–733.

Herbert A. Edelstein (1999). Introduction to Data Mining and Knowledge Discovery, Third Edition, Two Crows Corporation.

Hlavica, C., Hülsberg, F. M., & Klapproth, U. (2017). Tax Fraud & Forensic Accounting - Umgang mit Wirtschaftskriminalität (2nd ed.). Springer Fachmedien Wiesbaden.

Hofmann, S. (2008). Handbuch Anti-Fraud-Management / Bilanzbetrug erkennen – vorbeugen – bekämpfen. Erich Schmidt Verlag GmbH & Co.

Hsu, C.-W., Chang, C.-C., & Lin, C.-J. (2016). A Practical Guide to Support Vector Classification. Department of Computer Sciences.

Huang, C.-M., Lee, Y.-J., Lin, D. K. J., & Huang, S.-Y. (2007). Model selection for support vector machines via uniform design. Computational Statistics & Data Analysis, 52, 335–346.

Huang, C. L., & Wang, C. J. (2006). A GA-based feature selection and parameters optimizationfor support vector machines. Expert Systems with Applications, 31(2), 231–240.

Huang, J., Lu, J., & Ling, C. X. (2003). Comparing naive Bayes, decision trees, and SVM with AUC and accuracy. Third IEEE International Conference on Data Mining, 11–14.

Humpherys, S. L., Moffitt, K. C., Burns, M. B., Burgoon, J. K., & Felix, W. F. (2011). Identification of fraudulent financial statements using linguistic credibility analysis. Decision Support Systems, 50(3), 585–594.

International Planned Parenthood Federation (2009). IPPF – Practice Guide: Internal Auditing and Fraud. Retrieved from https://www.louisiana.edu/sites/auditor/files-/1011919_2029.dl_PG IA and Fraud.pdf (viewed on 12th August 2017).

Jans, M., Lybaert, N., & Vanhoof, K. (2009). A Framework for Internal Fraud Risk Reduction at IT Integrating Business Processes: The IFR^2 Framework. The International Journal of Digital Accounting Research, 9, 1–29.

Joshi, R. (2016) Accuracy, Precision, Recall & F1 Score: Interpretation of Performance Measures, Internet article, Exsilo, published on 2016 August, from http://blog.exsilio.com/all/accuracy-precision-recall-f1-score-interpretation-of-performance-measures/ (viewed on 13th September 2017)

Kajaree, D., & Behera, R. . (2017). A Survey on Machine Learning: Concept, Algorithms and Applications. International Journal of Innovative Research in Computer and Communication Engineering, 5(2), 1302–1309.

Kao, A., & Poteet, R. S. (Eds). (2007). Natural language processing and text mining. Springer Science & Business Media.

Karatzoglou, A., Meyer, D., & Hornik, K. (2005). Support Vector Machines in R. Research Report Series / Department of Statistics and Mathematics, WU Vienna University, 21.

Kehl, T., (2017). Geldwäsche einfach erklärt! – Mit vielen anschaulichen Beispielen. Retrieved from http://www.finanzfluss.de/was-ist-geldwasche/ (viewed 19th July 2017)

Kibekbaev, A., & Duman, E. (2016). Profit-Based Logistic Regression Trained By Migrating Birds Optimization : a Case Study in Credit Card Fraud Detection, (c), 148–155.

Kirkos, E., Spathis, C., & Manolopoulos, Y. (2007). Data Mining techniques for the detection of fraudulent financial statements. Expert Systems with Applications, 32(4), 995–1003.

KPMG. (2016). Tatort Deutschland - Wirtschaftskriminalität in Deutschland 2016 Studie. Retrieved from https://assets.kpmg.com/content/dam/kpmg/pdf/2016/07/-wirtschaftskriminalitaet-2016-2-KPMG.pdf (viewed on 12th August 2017).

Lani, J., (n.d.). What is Logisitc Regression, Internet Blog, Statistic Solutions. Retrieved from http://www.statisticssolutions.com/what-is-logistic-regression/ (viewed on 11th September 2017).

Largeron, C., Moulin, C., & Géry, M. (2011). Entropy based feature selection for text categorization. In Proceedings of the ACM Symposium on Applied Computing (pp. 924–928). ACM.

Le, Q. V, Coates, A., Prochnow, B., & Ng, A. Y. (2011). On Optimization Methods for Deep Learning. Proceedings of The 28th International Conference on Machine Learning (ICML), 265–272.

Lemon, S. C., Roy, J., Clark, M. A., Friedmann, P. D., & Rakowski, W. (2003). Classification and Regression Tree Analysis in Public Health: Methodological Review and Comparison With Logistic Regression. Ann Behav Med, 26(3), 172–181.

Lo (2013). Differences between L1 and L2 as Loss Function and Regularization. Internet article, published on 2013 December. Retrieved from http://www.chioka.in/differences-between-l1-and-l2-as-loss-function-and-regularization/ (viewed on 28th September 2017).

Lescher, G., & Baldeweg, R. (2012). Abrechnungsbetrug im Gesundheitswesen. Retrieved from http://www.pwc.de/gesundheitswesen (viewed on 15th August 2017).

Liebl, D. P. K. (2016). Wirtschafts- und Organisierte Kriminalität. Journal of Chemical Information and Modeling (Vol. 53).

LII (n.d.). Health Care Fraud: An Overview, Cornell Law School. Retrieved from https://www.law.cornell.edu/wex/healthcare_fraud (viewed on 14th August 2017).

Lin, C. C., Chiu, A. A., Huang, S. Y., & Yen, D. C. (2015). Detecting the financial statement fraud: The analysis of the differences between data mining techniques and experts' judgments. Knowledge-Based Systems, 89, 459–470.

Lloyd, S., Mohseni, M., & Rebentrost, P. (2013). Quantum algorithms for supervised and unsupervised machine learning. Massachusetts Institute of Technology, Research Laboratory for Electronics, 1–11.

Mahmud, M. S., Meesad, P., & Sodsee, S. (2016). An evaluation of computational intelligence in credit card fraud detection. In 2016 International Computer Science and Engineering Conference (ICSEC) 1-6.

Markham, K., (2014). Simple guide to confusion matrix terminology, Internet article, Data School, published on 2014 March. Retrieved from http://www.dataschool.io/simple-guide-to-confusion-matrix-terminology/ (viewed on 13th September 2017).

McAfee, A. & Brynjolfsson, E. (2012). Big Data: The Management Revolution. Harvard Business Review, 90(10), 61-68.

Miner, G. D., Delen, D., Elder, J., Fast, A., Hill, T., & Nisbet, R. A. (2012). Practical text mining and statistical analysis for non-structured text data applications. Waltham, MA : Academic Press (1st ed.).

More, A. (2016). Survey of resampling techniques for improving classification performance in unbalanced datasets. arXiv preprint arXiv:1608.06048.

Moro, S., & Laureano, R. M. S. (2011). Using Data Mining for Bank Direct Marketing: An application of the CRISP-DM methodology. European Simulation and Modelling Conference, (Figure 1), 117–121.

Nadali, A., Kakhky, E. N., & Nosratabadi, H. E. (2011). Evaluating the success level of data mining projects based on CRISP-DM methodology by a Fuzzy expert system. ICECT 2011 - 2011 3rd International Conference on Electronics Computer Technology, 6, 161–165.

New York Post (2017). Credit card fraud alerts are on the rise – save yourself. Retrieved from https://nypost.com/2017/05/12/credit-card-fraud-alerts-are-on-the-rise-save-yourself/ (viewed on 31th October 2017).

Ng, A. Y. (2004). Feature selection, L1 vs. L2 regularization, and rotational invariance. Twenty-First International Conference on Machine Learning - ICML '04, 78.

Ngai, E. W. T., Xiu, L., & Chau, D. C. K. (2009). Expert Systems with Applications Application of data mining techniques in customer relationship management : A literature review and classification. Expert Systems With Applications, 36(2), 2592–2602.

Ngai, E.W.T., Hu, Y., Wong, Y. H., Chen, Y., & Sun, X. (2010). The application of data mining techniques in financial fraud detection: A classification framework and an academic review of literature, Decision Support System, 50(3), 559-569.

Ngai, E. W. T., Hu, Y., Wong, Y. H., Chen, Y., & Sun, X. (2011). The application of data mining techniques in financial fraud detection: A classification framework and an academic review of literature. Decision Support Systems, 50(3), 559–569.

NHCAA (n.d.). The Challenge of Health Care Fraud. Retrieved from https://www.nhcaa.org/resources/health-care-anti-fraud-resources/the-challenge-of-health-care-fraud.aspx (viewed 14th August 2017).

Nilson. (2016). The Nilson Report, (1096). Retrieved from https://www.nilsonreport.com/upload/content_promo/The_Nilson_Report_10-17-2016.pdf

Olson, R. S., La Cava, W., Mustahsan, Z., Varik, A., & Moore, J. H. (2017). Data-driven Advice for Applying Machine Learning to Bioinformatics Problems.

Oxford University Press (2017). Concise Oxford English Dictionary. Retrieved from https://en.oxforddictionaries.com/definition/fraud (viewed 07th August 2017).

Pandey, N., Sanyal, D. K., Hudait, A., & Sen, A. (2017). Automated classification of software issue reports using machine learning techniques: an empirical study. Innovations in Systems and Software Engineering, pp. 1–19.

Peng, Y., Wang, G., Kou, G., & Shi, Y. (2011). An empirical study of classification algorithm evaluation for financial risk prediction. Applied Soft Computing, 11(2), 2906–2915.

Pfeifer, K. (2014). Serviceorientiertes Text Mining am Beispiel von Entitätsextrahierenden Diensten. Technischen Universität Dresden.

Potamitis, G. (2013). Design and Implementation of a Fraud Detection Expert System using Ontology- Based Techniques. University of Manchester.

Powers, D. M. W. (2011). Evaluation: from Precision, Recall and F-measure to ROC, Informedness, Markedness and Correlation. Journal of Machine Learning Technologies, 2(1), 37–63.

Qamar, U. (2016). Text Mining Approach to Detect Spam in Emails. In Proceedings of The International Conference on Innovations in Intelligent Systems and Computing Technologies.

Raschka, S. (n.d.). Why are implementations of decision tree algorithms usually binary and what are the advantages of the different impurity metrics? Internet article. Retrieved from https://sebastianraschka.com/faq/docs/decision-tree-binary.html (viewed on 28th September 2017).

Raschka, S. (2016). Model evaluation, model selection, and algorithm selection in machine learning - Part III - Cross-validation and hyperparameter tuning, Internet article, published on 2016 October. Retrieved from https://sebastianraschka.com/blog/2016/model-evaluation-selection-part3.html (viewed on 22th September 2017).

Rashid Al-Azmi, A.-A. (2013). Data, Text and Web Mining for Business Intelligence : A Survey. International Journal of Data Mining & Knowledge Management Process, 3(2), 1–21.

Robertson, S. (2004). Understanding inverse document frequency: on theoretical arguments for IDF. Journal of Documentation, 60(5), 503–520.

Rocha, B., & Júnior, R. (2010). Identifying Bank Frauds Using Crisp-Dm and Decision Trees. International Journal of Computer Science & Information Technology (IJCSIT), 2(5),

162–169.

Rouce, M., (2016) Data Sampling (Datenauswahl), Internet Definition, TechTarget, published on 2016 November. Retrieved from http://www.searchenterprisesoftware.de/definition/Data-Sampling-Datenauswahl (viewed on 19th September 2017)

Sabbah, T., Selamat, A., Selamat, M. H., Al-Anzi, F. S., Viedma, E. H., Krejcar, O., & Fujita, H. (2017). Modified frequency-based term weighting schemes for text classification. Applied Soft Computing Journal, 58, 193–206.

Salinger, L. (2004). Encyclopedia of White Collar and Corporate Crime. Sage Pubn, 2,179–181.

Salton, G., Wong, A. and Yang, C. S. (1975). A vector space model for automatic indexing. Communations of the ACM, 18(11).

Salvenmoser, S., Nestler, C., (n.d.). Prävention von Wirtschaftskriminalität: Deutsche Unternehmen mit Defiziten, PwC Article and Interview, published by PwC. Retrieved from https://www.pwc.de/de/risiko-management/praevention-von-wirtschaftskriminalitaet-deutsche-unternehmen-mit-defiziten.html (viewed on 19th July 2017).

Scherp, D. (2015). Fraud Management - Abwehr von Kriminalität in der Organisation von Kreditinstituten und Finanzdienstleistern (2. Auflage). Bank-Verlag.

Schramm, H., Litzel, N. (2012). Strukturierte und Unstrukturierte Daten effizient verwalten, Internet article, published by Vogel Business Media. Retrieved from http://www.storage-insider.de/strukturierte-und-unstrukturierte-daten-effizient-verwalten-a-369015/ (viewed on 31th August 2017).

Schuchter, A. (2012). Perspektiven verurteilter Wirtschaftsstraftäter - Gründe ihrer Handlungen und Prävention in Unternehmen (1st ed.). Gabler Verlag.

Seeja, K. R., & Zareapoor, M. (2014). FraudMiner: A Novel Credit Card Fraud Detection Model Based on Frequent Itemset Mining. The Scientific World Journal, 2014, 1–10.

Shafique, U., & Qaiser, H. (2014). A Comparative Study of Data Mining Process Models (KDD , CRISP-DM and SEMMA). International Journal of Innovation and Scientific Research, 12(1), 217–222.

Sharafi, A. (2013). Knowledge Discovery in Databases - Eine Analyse des Änderungsmanagement in der Produktentwicklung. Springer Gabler.

Sharma, V., & Pandey, B. (2015). Importance of Unstructured Data in Financial Fraud Detection. Thirteenth AIMS International Conference on Management, At Bangalore, India.

Shaw, M. J., Subramaniam, C., Tan, G. W., & Welge, M. E. (2001). Knowledge management and data mining for marketing. Decision Support Systems, 31(1), 127-137.

Shearer, C., Watson, H. J., Grecich, D. G., Moss, L., Adelman, S., Hammer, K., & Herdlein, S. a. (2000). The CRISP-DM model: The New Blueprint for Data Mining. Journal of Data Warehousing, 5(4), 13–22.

Singleton, T., & Singleton, A. J. (2010). Fraud Auditing and Forensic Accounting (4th ed.). Wiley.

Sorin, A. (2012). Survey of Clustering based Financial Fraud Detection Research. Informatica Economica, 16(1), 110–123.

Soukup T., (2002). Visual Data Mining: Techniques and Tools for Data Visualization and Mining (Computer Science), John Wiley & Sons, 1.

Spiegel Online (2017). Top Manager verursachen Großteil der Wirtschaftskriminalität. Retrieved from http://www.spiegel.de/wirtschaft/unternehmen/studie-top-manager-verursachen-grossteil-der-wirtschaftskriminalitaet-a-793889.html (viewed on 31th October 2017).

Srivastava, N., Hinton, G., Krizhevsky, A., Sutskever, I., & Salakhutdinov, R. (2014). Dropout: A Simple Way to Prevent Neural Networks from Overfitting. Journal of Machine Learning Research, 15, 1929–1958.

Stadler, W. A., & Lovrich, N. P. (2012). Special Sensitivity? : The White-Collar Offender in Prison (1st ed.). LFB Scholarly Publishing LLC.

Sutherland, E. H. (1983). White collar crime : the uncut version / Edwin H. Sutherland ; with and introduction by Gilbert Geis and Colin Goff. New Haven Yale University Press, 1983.

Talib, R., Hanif, M. K., Ayesha, S., & Fatima, F. (2016). Text Mining: Techniques, Applications and Issues. IJACSA) International Journal of Advanced Computer Science and Applications, 7(11).

Tartakovsky, S., Clark, S. and McCourt, M. (2017). Deep Learning Hyperparameter Optimization with Competing Objectives, Internet Source, published on 2017 August. Retrieved from https://devblogs.nvidia.com/parallelforall/sigopt-deep-learning-hyperparameter-optimization/ (viewed on 23th September 2017).

Techmeier, I. (2012). Das Verhältnis von Kriminalität und Ökonomie-Eine empirische Studie am Beispiel der Privatisierung ehemaliger DDR-Betriebe. VS Verlag für Sozialwissenschaften, 1.

TID, (n.d.). Was ist Korruption? Transparancy International Deutschland e. V. Retireved from https://www.transparency.de/ueber-uns/was-ist-korruption/ (viewed 22th July 2017).

Tong, S., & Koller, D. (2001). Support Vector Machine Active Learning with Applications to

Text Classification. Journal of Machine Learning Research, 45–66.

Undhad, P. R., & Bhalodiya, D. J. (2017). Text Classification and Classifiers: A Comparative Study. International Journal of Engineering Development and Research, 5(2), 2321–9939.

Vafeiadis, T., Diamantaras, K. I., Sarigiannidis, G., & Chatzisavvas, K. C. (2015). A comparison of machine learning techniques for customer churn prediction. Simulation Modelling Practice and Theory, 55, 1–9.

Van Rijmenam, M. (2015). Why The 3V's Are Not Sufficient to Describe Big Data, published on 2015 Octover. Retrieved from https://vanrijmenam.nl/3vs-sufficient-describe-big-data/ (viewed on 30th August 2017).

Vishal Gupta, G. S. L. (2009). A Survey of Text Mining Techniques and Applications. Journal of Emerging Technologies in Web Intelligence, 1(1), 17.

Warren, J. & Marz, N., 2015. Big Data Principles and best practices of scalable real-time data systems, Shelter Island: Manning Publications Co.

Weiss, S. M., Indurkhya, N., & Zhang, T. (2010). Fundamentals of Predictive Text Mining. Springer, London.

West, J., & Bhattacharya, M. (2016). Intelligent financial fraud detection: A comprehensive review. School of Computing & Mathematics, Charles Sturt University, Albury, NSW 2640,Australia, Computers and Security, 57, 47-66.

Wieland, U., & Fischer, M. (2013). Zur Methodischen Vorbereitung von Data-Mining-Projekten Unter Verwendung von CRISP-DM im Kontext Diskreter Produktionsprozesse. CEUR Workshop Proceedings, 1049, 47–63.

Witten, I. H., Eibe Frank, M., Hall, A., & Pal, C. J. (2016). Data Mining: Practical Machine Learning Tools and Techniques (4th ed.). Morgan Kaufmann.

Wolfhart Nitsch, K. (2014). Handbuch des Insolvenzrechts. 1st edn. Europaeischer Hochschulver-lag

Wu, C.-H., Tzeng, G.-H., & Lin, R.-H. (2009). A Novel hybrid genetic algorithm for kernel function and parameter optimization in support vector regression. Expert Systems with Applications, 36(3), 4725–4735.

Yaram, S. (2016). Machine learning algorithms for document clustering and fraud detection. 2016 International Conference on Data Science and Engineering (ICDSE), 1–6.

Yoo, I., Alafaireet, P., Marinov, M., Pena-Hernandez, K., Gopidi, R., Chang, J. F., & Hua, L. (2012). Data mining in healthcare and biomedicine: A survey of the literature. Journal of Medical Systems, 36(4), 2431–2448.

Zanaty, E. A. (2012). Support Vector Machines (SVMs) versus Multilayer Perception (MLP) in data classification. Egyptian Informatics Journal, 13(3), 177–183.

Zareapoor, M., Seeja.K.R, S. K. ., & Afshar Alam, M. (2012). Analysis on Credit Card Fraud Detection Techniques: Based on Certain Design Criteria. International Journal of Computer Applications, 52(3), 35–42.

Zawlilla, P., Lamboy, C. de, & Jackmuth, H.-W. (2012). Fraud Management: Der Mensch als Schlüsselfaktor gegen Wirtschaftskriminalität (1st ed.). Frankfurt School Verlag.

Zhang, D., & Zhou, L. (2004). Discovering golden nuggets: data mining in financial application, IEEE Transactions on Systems, Man and Cybernetics.

Zhuoyuan, Z., Yunpeng, C., & Ye, L. (2015). Oversampling method for imbalanced classification. Computing and Informatics, 5(34), 1017-1037.

YOUR KNOWLEDGE HAS VALUE